God's Word, Our Story

Other Books by the Gospel Coalition

Don't Call It a Comeback: The Old Faith for a New Day, edited by Kevin DeYoung

Entrusted with the Gospel: Pastoral Expositions of 2 Timothy, edited by D. A. Carson

God's Love Compels Us: Taking the Gospel to the World, edited by D. A. Carson and Kathleen B. Nielson

The Gospel as Center: Renewing Our Faith and Reforming Our Ministry Practices, edited by D. A. Carson and Timothy Keller

Here Is Our God: God's Revelation of Himself in Scripture, edited by Kathleen B. Nielson and D. A. Carson

His Mission: Jesus in the Gospel of Luke, edited by D. A. Carson and Kathleen B. Nielson

The Scriptures Testify about Me: Jesus and the Gospel in the Old Testament, edited by D. A. Carson

The Gospel Coalition Booklets
Edited by D. A. Carson and Timothy Keller

Baptism and the Lord's Supper, by Thabiti M. Anyabwile and J. Ligon Duncan

Can We Know the Truth?, by Richard D. Phillips

Christ's Redemption, by Sandy Willson

The Church: God's New People, by Timothy Savage

Creation, by Andrew M. Davis

The Gospel and Scripture: How to Read the Bible, by Mike Bullmore

Gospel-Centered Ministry, by D. A. Carson and Timothy Keller

The Holy Spirit, by Kevin L. DeYoung

Justification, by Philip Graham Ryken

The Kingdom of God, by Stephen T. Um

The Plan, by Colin S. Smith

The Restoration of All Things, by Sam Storms

Sin and the Fall, by Reddit Andrews III

What Is the Gospel?, by Bryan Chapell

God's Word, Our Story

Learning from the Book of Nehemiah

D. A. CARSON

AND

KATHLEEN B. NIELSON,

EDITORS

WHEATON, ILLINOIS

Library of Congress Cataloging-in-Publication Data
Names: Carson, D. A., editor.
Title: God's word, our story : learning from the Book of Nehemiah / D.A.
     Carson and Kathleen Nielson, editors.
Description: Wheaton : Crossway, 2016. | "The Gospel Coalition." |
     Includes bibliographical references and index.
Identifiers: LCCN 2015034170 | ISBN 9781433549694 (tp)
Subjects: LCSH: Bible. Nehemiah—Criticism, interpretation, etc.
Classification: LCC BS1365.52 .G63 2016 | DDC 222/.806—dc23
LC record available at http://lccn.loc.gov/2015034170

Contents

Foreword

Nehemiah is one of my favorite books in the Bible. I've taught through it many times. In these thirteen chapters, we are shown how greatly God cares for his city, his people, his kingdom. During one of the lowest moments in our history as God's people, he raised up an extraordinary servant to accomplish the daunting task of rebuilding the city walls and the people within those walls. We grant that Nehemiah is one of the Bible's finest champions, but God himself is the ultimate and only hero of this, and every, biblical book.

I commend this book to you. Kathleen Nielson drew together outstanding expositors, who addressed attentive thousands at The Gospel Coalition Women's Conference in June 2014, and whose written expositions will now serve many more who want to learn from God's Word and learn more about studying and teaching God's Word. At the conclusion of every exposition, Kathleen has assembled sage advice for those who would teach the text.

One of the chief concerns of The Gospel Coalition has always been faithful, intelligent, Spirit-empowered, gospel-centered exposition of the sacred Scriptures. From our very earliest meetings as TGC Council members, we prayerfully discussed how we might encourage our sisters in the Lord, just as we wanted to strengthen our brothers in the Lord. But I think none of us imagined what a powerful and fruitful ministry would one day rise up under Kathleen's remarkable leadership. The regional training events planned for ensuing years, in which women leaders in local churches will be diligently trained to teach the Scriptures and to teach others how to do so, will expand this great work even further, as part of the ongoing ministry of TGC's women's initiatives.

We will all be the wiser for studying each of the chapters in this book, in order that we may serve the church and the world through faithful biblical exposition.

Sandy Willson
Senior minister, Second Presbyterian Church, Memphis, TN
Founding member of TGC Council

Introduction

On Exposition

Kathleen Nielson

Why, some people ask, do we devote so many hours at a Gospel Coalition conference to those huge plenary sessions, where one person stands up front and talks? Ours is an interactive age, and people aren't used to listening for such long periods; couldn't we cut a few of those talks?

Not really, and here's why. The Gospel Coalition is one of those ministries that holds the preaching and teaching of God's Word as centrally important. And we want that importance to show in our conferences—especially in an age when expository preaching is less and less valued.

This collection of talks from The Gospel Coalition's 2014 National Women's Conference (TCGW14) is a bit different from previous collections. Our aim in this volume is not just to share the talks, but also, in the process, to encourage readers to think about the nature and value of biblical exposition. We'd love for readers to be not only inspired by reading these messages on Nehemiah, but also better equipped to do the kind of study and preparation that would enable them to expound the Word themselves—

perhaps to large audiences, to Bible study groups, to children, or to a friend over coffee.

To that end, we've included after each chapter not only reflection questions but also a few comments, including personal comments from the contributors, on the process of studying and preparing; these "Think Like an Expositor" sections focus on just one or two particular aspects of teaching that text. The conclusion looks back and reflects on the work of digging into Old Testament narrative in particular. The whole book, then, is an initial exploration of the *how* of exposition, through the various voices of these experienced Bible teachers. This introduction begins the conversation by asking three basic questions about biblical exposition: *What? Why?* and *Where?*

The *What* of Biblical Exposition

What do we mean by *biblical exposition*? The term is used quite often, and sometimes loosely, within the evangelical world. *Exposition* traditionally means some kind of public display—a "placing out," according to the root meaning of the word, as in a museum's exposition of a valuable collection. The items in the collection are laid out in an exhibit that allows people to take in the treasures that are there. That's what biblical exposition is, at its heart: not creating new treasures—or decorating the old ones—but laying out the Word treasures that are there and helping people see them clearly in the form in which we're given them—that is, passage by passage and book by book, within the Scriptures of the Old and New Testaments.

Among those who embrace expositional teaching, various definitions (and various strategies) can be found. One helpful, succinct definition comes from Pastor David Helm: "Expositional preaching is empowered preaching that rightfully submits the shape and emphasis of the sermon to the shape and emphasis of a biblical text."[1]

---

[1] David Helm, *Expositional Preaching: How We Speak God's Word Today* (Wheaton, IL: Crossway, 2014), 13.

In other words, an expositor's main job is not to expound an idea or ideas taken from a text; it is not to expound the present culture in relation to a text; and it is not to expound an argument supported by various fragments of texts. An expositor's job is to *expound a text* of Scripture by bringing to light its whole form and content—and not simply as an academic exercise: notice these words in Helm's definition: "empowered" and "rightfully submits." The power of exposition comes not simply from right answers about the text and certainly not from a powerful personality that gets the text across, but from a right and full submission to the powerful Spirit of God who breathed out the Bible's living and active words, who dwells in the Christian preacher or teacher, and who actively helps him or her rightly to articulate the meaning of the words in the text so that they penetrate hearts as they are intended to do, for the glory of Christ.

The *Why* of Biblical Exposition

We understand the *what* even better when we begin to ask the *why* of biblical exposition. Why is it so important to expound Scripture—to lay it out clearly, to let its shape and emphasis be the shape and emphasis we offer to our listeners? I will offer five reasons, but the list is not exhaustive. I recommend exploration of the various publications and authors noted in this introduction in order to study more exhaustively all sorts of questions relating to biblical exposition.

First, *biblical exposition is so important because the Bible is God speaking.* If we had to choose just one reason, this, of course, would be it. If it is true that these words are God-breathed (2 Tim. 3:16), written by men who "spoke from God as they were carried along by the Holy Spirit" (2 Pet. 1:21), then nothing is more important than hearing these words clearly. The One who spoke these words made us. He also made a way to save us from his wrath, which we in our sin deserve. He loves us and lights the way to him. That way is found in his Word. That way is Jesus, who is at the center of this Word. Hearing this Word clearly and truly is a life-and-death matter. Submitting to God's Word as to the Lord himself is what we human beings were created to do, for his glory and for our good. When a person stands up to handle the Word of the God of the universe, eternal realities are at stake.

These realities are personal, not abstract. God's Word is alive and active because God is alive and active. Sometimes we actually forget he is there as we receive and discuss his words to us. Pastor Mike Bullmore offers a great reminder: "Preacher, imagine God sitting in the congregation as you preach. What will be the expression on his face? Will it say, 'That's not at all what I was getting at with that passage.' Or will it say, 'Yes that's exactly what I intended.'"[2]

Second, *biblical exposition is so important because it gives us confidence in our message.* The above quotation from Pastor Bullmore can be a little scary. When we're honest, we redeemed believers know our sins and limitations that regularly impede our teaching. We know we're fully capable of missing what God is getting at, or perhaps being guided by our own concerns and perspectives more than by deep study of and submission to the actual text. We all miss the expositional mark regularly. Please be sure that we do not offer these talks on Nehemiah as perfect examples. (I think I can speak for all the contributors!) They are humbly offered as examples, conceived with the aim of pleasing God by letting people hear as clearly as possible his life-giving words.

The kind of confidence we're talking about is a humble confidence developed through Word study that is not disconnected from personal communion with the God who spoke it. This communion is known only through Christ, who by his death and resurrection made that communion possible. It is encouraging that, as we dare to teach, we believers in Christ have the best help possible: not only his people around us, but his own Holy Spirit with us and in us to help us take in the words he breathed out. In a chapter that

---

[2] Mike Bullmore, "A Biblical Case for Expositional Preaching," 9marks, Feb. 25, 2010, http://9marks.org/article/biblical-case-expositional-preaching/ (accessed June 11, 2015).

offers a most excellent summary of "The Hermeneutical Distinctives of Expository Preaching," David Jackman comments on the importance of prayer as "central to the process of preparation": "We are entirely dependent on God's Spirit to open our blind eyes, unstop our deaf ears, and soften our hardened hearts, so at every stage in preparing to preach we seek the author's help to rightly hear and handle his Word of truth."[3] For years, my husband and I, along with our children, sat under the expository preaching of Pastor Kent Hughes, who consistently pointed his congregation to a full awareness of the triune God's presence as the Word was preached; that was a great gift.[4]

Our confidence comes ultimately from a personal trust in the first reason why biblical exposition is so important: that this is indeed God's Word—God speaking. We are aiming to lay out for people not our own wisdom from inside of ourselves, but the wisdom of words that come down to us like the rain and the snow from heaven, watering the earth, bringing fruit, accomplishing that which God purposes (Isa. 55:10–11). We don't have to rely on our wit, our rhetorical ability, or our winsome presence—although God can use all those things if he so chooses (the contributors to this volume have various and generous doses of those gifts). What we trust finally, though, is that what we have to offer, by God's grace, is sure, unfailing, beautiful, and effective—his Word. Our job is to get out of the way and let it speak (or, rather, let God speak, by his Spirit). These words are alive with the breath of God.

In his book *Preaching: Communicating Faith in an Age of Skepticism*, Tim Keller offers an extremely helpful initial discussion of the call to "Word ministry" on multiple levels—clearly establishing the basic principle that those who teach the Bible

---

[3] In *Preach the Word: Essays on Expository Preaching: In Honor of R. Kent Hughes*, ed. Leland Ryken and Todd Wilson (Wheaton, IL: Crossway, 2007), 9–21.

[4] See the Preaching the Word commentary series (Wheaton, IL: Crossway), many volumes of which Kent Hughes wrote, and every volume of which includes his Foreword, "A Word to Those Who Preach the Word," in which he talks about knowing the presence and the pleasure of God while preaching. A fuller discussion can be found in his "Anatomy of Exposition: *Logos*, *Ethos*, and *Pathos*," first delivered as part of the Mullins Lectures at the Southern Baptist Theological Seminary (1998) and available at http://www.simeontrust.org/media/doc-khughes-anatomy.pdf.

in any context must faithfully present God's words. Keller takes us to 1 Peter 4:10–11 and to Peter Davids's instructive thoughts on that passage, in which the apostle Peter admonishes anyone who speaks to "do so as one who speaks the very words of God" (NIV).[5] In doing so, we can trust his words to do his work, by his Spirit.

Third, *biblical exposition is so important because those who preach or teach should be guides, not gurus.* This point is obviously related to the last one. Because our confidence is in the Word itself, by the Spirit, we must aim to teach that confidence to others as we share the Word. We want to communicate not how much we have found in the text, but how much is to be found in the text— and, in the process, a bit about how to find it. We don't want listeners to go away saying, "Wow, what a good speaker. She's amazing. I never could have found all that in there"—but rather, "Wow, that was an amazing passage of Scripture. It struck my heart. I loved seeing how it holds together and fits into the whole book. I never thought about how directly it relates to Christ and to the gospel. I think I'll try asking some of those same questions of this other text I'm studying . . ."

Maybe that sounds a little ambitious or contrived. But, again, maybe not. Maybe that's really what we should be after. Don't we want to send people away marveling at God himself, moved to follow him more closely, lifting up his Son more wholeheartedly? In one sense, it's easier just to try to be witty or winsome and to pull a group of listeners along by those means. In another sense, it's much harder and more pressure-filled to make the message depend on *me*. In the end, I want my listeners to be protected from me! We want our listeners to follow us, yes—but to follow us in the way of his commandments, in the delightful path of his testimonies (Ps. 119:24, 32). We want to be guides, not gurus.

---

[5] *Preaching: Communicating Faith in an Age of Skepticism* (New York: Viking, 2015), 2–4. In this discussion, Keller references P. H. Davids, *The First Epistle of Peter* (Grand Rapids, MI: Eerdmans, 1990), 161.

Fourth, *biblical exposition is so important because regular expository teaching tells God's story truly.* Biblical exposition works through passages of Scripture in context. Most pastors who are biblical expositors preach through biblical books, passage after passage and week after week, so that their congregations receive God's Word in the form he ordained: in books, and in the collections of books we know as the Old and New Testaments. Many of these pastors, along with their elders, have made sure that this commitment to expository teaching trickles down through all the groups and programs in the church—so that a women's Bible study, for example, also is working regularly through books of the Old and New Testament. This is not to say that from time to time there isn't a great topical talk or series of talks. It is to say that the regular diet of Scripture intake consists of the whole Word of God, whole book by whole book.

We take in the Word in whole books because that is the form in which God has delivered his Word to us. He's made us a "people of the book." Even though in this day we all tend to be people of topics and snippets of information digested through one quick link after another, we must respect the beautiful coherence of the book we call the Bible. If an artist presented us with a magnificent sculpture, we probably would not feel free to break it apart and decorate our houses with one piece of it here and another fragment of it there. What if the artist visited us and saw his work of art torn to pieces? Now, it is certainly true that a topical or a nonexpositional Bible talk can do either a good or a bad job of respecting the coherence of Scripture. I would venture to guess that, if it does a good job, there's a good chance the speaker has spent time doing some background work in biblical exposition related to the verse or verses mentioned in that talk. Occasionally, a nonexpositor has so satiated himself or herself in the whole of Scripture that one part naturally and beautifully resonates with another.

The Bible is God's work of art. Each book's form and content, and the unity of the whole Bible, represent an unparalleled literary masterpiece, with multiple genres combining to speak one unified story. It's the universal story, the true story of the universe. It's God's telling of his redemption of a people for himself for his glory, through his Son. We like to summarize the arc of that story in four parts, as several of our TGCW14 speakers mention: creation, fall, redemption, and consummation. Every book, from Genesis to Revelation, finds its place and its ultimate meaning within that big story. And every passage within every book finds its meaning as part of that whole book and as part of the whole story.

There's no other way to get the story right than to listen to it the way God tells it. There's no other way to delight fully in the story than to contemplate it in its fullness. We deepen our knowledge of Jesus Christ, the Son of God and the Savior of the world, as we grasp his part in the story from the very beginning (in creation) to the very end (at his second coming and into eternity). The cross and resurrection that are the climax at the center of the story cannot be torn away from the beginning and the end—and all the other parts in between. Every passage of Scripture finds its fullness of revelation in the gospel of Jesus Christ; as Charles Haddon Spurgeon famously taught, just as from every town, village, and hamlet in England there is a road to London, "so from every text of Scripture there is a road to Christ."[6] In him are life and light, from the story's start to finish. To know and to grow in Christ, we need to know God's Word.

We may think that one topic and one verse on that topic are the most relevant stuff to offer the group we're leading or speaking to, but in the end, the most relevant message we can offer is consistent teaching through the Word of God, by which God's Spirit reveals God himself to us. And God is eternally relevant. We all think we know what we need to hear; God knew it from the beginning, and if we keep listening to his voice through his Word, we'll keep getting to the topics we need to have addressed (some of which

---

[6] Charles Haddon Spurgeon, "Christ Precious to Believers," sermon at Music Hall, Royal Surrey Gardens, March 13, 1859, http://www.spurgeon.org/sermons/0242.htm (accessed June 17, 2015).

we didn't know we needed). We will address these topics through passages we study in their contexts before we jump to our own contexts. We will discover a beautiful network of roads to Christ. And, in giving careful attention to God's story the way he tells it, we will find our individual stories within it.

These talks on the book of Nehemiah have been exciting to so many because they uncover an amazing part of the story that not only connects beautifully to the whole Bible, but also connects with each of our own parts in the story right now. This story of returning exiles is our history as the people of God, and he is the same God yesterday, today, and forever—working out his eternal plan of redemption through his Son. It is hugely encouraging to find whole-Bible connections and deeply personal connections in the chapters of Nehemiah, as we follow the story from the opening scene in the capital of the Persian Empire to the final scene in Jerusalem.

Fifth, *biblical exposition is so important because it grows us up into mature followers of Christ.* "Little-snippet teaching" is one way to stay on a milk diet forever instead of moving on to meat (see 1 Cor. 3:1–2). For one thing, exposition challenges our minds and hearts to take in the literary logic of the larger biblical story; we stretch our thoughts, for example, to take in the details of the first Passover celebration, and then connect the Passover with Jesus, the Lamb of God; we picture the Jerusalem temple in all its intricacy, and then see the picture come alive in Christ, who is our temple—and who then calls us to become living stones in a living temple; or we follow the train of thought through those Old Testament sacrifices, which covered sin, to the sacrifice of Christ, which washed it away. Scripture asks of us complex progressions of thought and imagination, and we become mature in every way as we submit to following the life-giving ways of the Word. God himself is infinite and gloriously holy; the gift of his Word allows us the privilege of beginning to delve into the glorious depths of knowing him. This privilege lets us practice for life in eternity.

We're not talking about knowledge just for the sake of pure knowledge, to be sure—although the kind of careful study involved in expository teaching will stretch any person intellectually. But biblical exposition is, at heart, about knowing God and making him known through his Word. First and foremost, the Word makes us "wise for salvation through faith in Christ Jesus" (2 Tim. 3:15). The kind of maturity the Word invites us to embrace, then, is a growing up in the Lord—in his ways, in his thoughts that are higher than ours, and ultimately in Christ, who is the full and perfect revelation of his Father. In knowing Jesus through the Word, we know and commune with God more and more deeply. In sharing the Word, we share not just knowledge about God; we share the living Christ. "Him we proclaim," declares the apostle Paul, "warning everyone and teaching everyone with all wisdom, that we may present everyone mature in Christ. For this I toil, struggling with all his energy that he powerfully works within me" (Col. 1:28–29).

Sharing the Word in this way happens among people. Expository teaching is not a solo performance to be isolated from a community. This is the problem, of course, with conferences that pull people out of their normal communities and eventually connect virtually with millions of people whom the speakers never see or know. The Gospel Coalition is a ministry intent on helping to build up the church; our goal is to send preachers, teachers, and church members back from our conferences (and from listening to these conferences) to their local congregations, encouraged and equipped to serve even more fruitfully there, among real, live people!

The scene in Nehemiah 8 gives a powerful picture of what it looks like when God's Word is expounded to God's people. This huge assembly of returned exiles—"men and women and all who could understand" (vv. 2, 3)—gathered in the square before the Water Gate and listened attentively for hours to the reading of the Law, while Levites moved among them, helping them understand:

"they gave the sense, so that the people understood the reading" (v. 8). They explained the words so that the people got the meaning. They expounded the Word to God's gathered people—who went away rejoicing "because they had understood the words that were declared to them" (v. 12).

Nehemiah goes on to show ongoing effects of the Word at work among God's people as it is explained and received with clear understanding and open hearts. Of course, part of what the people understood from the biblical exposition was the story of their sin and their need for a deliverer from that sin. The ongoing effects of that part of the story are evident as well, in subsequent chapters. And part of *our* understanding of Nehemiah is the part he and his people played in God's preparing of the way for the promised deliverer. The maturity required of all of us, at every point in redemptive history, comes from receiving and believing every word of God's delivered revelation of himself, as the Spirit enables us—which means, for us now, receiving and believing in Jesus Christ, the Son of God, the Word made flesh. The believing people God is creating for himself through his Son are the great *why* of biblical exposition.

Why is biblical exposition so important? Because the Bible is God speaking. Only as we expound his Word can we be confident in our message, serving as guides, not gurus, telling God's story truly so that people can know and grow up into Jesus Christ, God's Son.

The *Where* of Biblical Exposition

We've said that biblical exposition takes place among God's people. And we've used the terms *preaching* and *teaching* to refer to that activity practiced by both men and women. Where do women in particular fit in, in relation to the question of preaching and teaching? We at TGC joyfully and wholeheartedly affirm "the distinctive leadership role within the church given to qualified men," a role that, according to Scripture, is grounded in creation, fall, and redemption.[7] We also joyfully and wholeheartedly affirm that, along with the authoritative and teaching roles set apart for qualified men in the context of God's gathered people, there are more opportunities to teach God's Word in this wide world than all the women of the church together will ever be able to meet. Granted, among committed complementarians, there is not perfect unanimity concerning the hermeneutical significance of the conjunctions in 1 Timothy 2:12 or concerning certain contexts of teaching. We must all study hard and prayerfully, listen well, and articulate carefully—and we must do this in the context of the church, as members of Christ's body who worship and serve in local congregations where we can fully commit ourselves to respect the authority of the elders in leadership.

And we must encourage women to learn to teach the Bible and train them to do it! The opportunities to teach other women are huge today. These opportunities are not to be scorned in a scramble for other or wider audiences that might seem more desirable; there is a significant need for well-trained, articulate women who can expound Scripture well to other women who want to learn. Opportunities exist in Western settings, where women are increasingly hungry to learn from each other in substantive ways, within the clear context of church life and leadership. And opportunities exist in spades in non-Western settings—in many cases, where no man would ever be allowed to venture. As global connections and awareness grow, so should our hearts—to take the good news of the living Word to women in places where they have never heard, and into women's gatherings where only other women are able to infiltrate. Sometimes these gatherings are on the other side of the globe, and sometimes (often) they are just around a few corners from where we live.

Neither should we scorn opportunities to teach children, in both formal and informal contexts, shaping the whole trajectory

---

[7] See The Gospel Coalition's Foundation Documents: http://www.thegospelcoalition.org /about/foundation-documents

of human lives in the pathways of the Word. And many kinds of teaching take place less formally—in a small-group discussion, over tea, or perhaps in a Priscilla/Aquila-like session (Acts 18:24–26). I appreciate the clear message of authors already noted that the principles of biblical exposition are crucial for all teachers of the Bible, in multiple contexts.[8] In the end, every believer in Jesus Christ is called to study and share the Scriptures—to do Word ministry in all kinds of contexts. The *where* of biblical exposition for laypeople, including women, needs to grow and expand, as all God's people become more and more equipped to share the Word faithfully and well.

May this volume of talks from TGCW14 help to further that end! By God's grace, may we in the church be raising up many women and men who love the Word, who delight to lay out its treasures, and who encourage others to share those treasures through faithful biblical exposition, for the glory of Christ alone.

---

[8] Keller's *Preaching*, for example, emphasizes this point, recommending the same emphasis in the seminal work by Peter Adam, *Speaking God's Words: A Practical Theology of Preaching* (Vancouver, British Columbia: Regent College Publishing, 1996).

Taking Action in Light of God's Word

Nehemiah 1–2

Kathy Keller

As we begin the study of Nehemiah, will you take a minute to find this book in your Bible? Take a look at its location in the Old Testament. Did you find it right in the middle, just before you get to Psalms?

No, Nehemiah is *not* right in the middle. It's at the end. Now you're puzzled, because it looks like it's in the middle of your Old Testament. But Nehemiah is chronologically at the end of the Old Testament books recording the history of Israel. There's a lot more Scripture that follows it: the Wisdom Literature, the Psalms, the prophetic utterances. But in Nehemiah, we get the last glimpse of Old Testament history before the curtain comes down and the silence of four hundred years begins, only to be broken by the angels singing about the birth of the Messiah.

Nehemiah is an Old Testament narrative that shows God's people mercifully returning from exile in accordance with God's promises, but at a very great point of need. Israel is no longer a magnificent kingdom, but a weak, conquered remnant. The people are rebuilding a broken-down city under the leadership of a man whose only visible qualification is that he follows God.

Let's jump right into the text: Nehemiah 1 and 2. There is much to learn here for twenty-first-century believers who want to be faithful to God's Word. As we'll see, this narrative tells a story of understanding and trusting God's Word.

Setting the Scene

Living in New York City, you tend to meet people who know people who know people. So over the past year or so, especially around the season of summer blockbuster action movies, I've had an occasional thought of trying to connect with someone in the film industry and selling Nehemiah as the next action movie—although, given what Hollywood recently did to Noah, maybe not.

If we try to imagine Nehemiah as an action movie, here's how it might open: a dark, brooding shot pans the destroyed walls surrounding Jerusalem. The stones have tumbled down. The gates are just piles of firewood, still smoking. The inhabitants, a small and hardy collection of returned exiles, are weeping and grieving.

Quick cut to Susa, the location of King Artaxerxes's citadel. Kislev, the month, is flashed on the bottom of the screen. Hanani, whom Nehemiah refers to as a brother, rides up with several others on tired and weary mounts. Gasping for breath, swallowing much-needed water, Hanani reports to Nehemiah this fresh disaster.

This is not the destruction of the walls of Jerusalem that took place under King Nebuchadnezzar in 587 BC, when the Jews were first taken into exile. That's old news. That had happened seventy years before, as the prophets Isaiah and Jeremiah had foretold. The southern kingdom of Judah had fallen to pagan invaders, just as the northern kingdom of Israel had much earlier. Nebuchadnezzar, at the head of the Babylonian army, had invaded and taken Jerusalem, destroyed the temple, broken the walls, and taken the people into captivity.

But through all the years of exile, God's people had held on to the prophets' promises that there would be an eventual restoration. Isaiah 44:28 gives God's words specifically about King Cyrus ("He is my shepherd, and he shall fulfill all my purpose"), about Jerusalem ("She shall be built"), and about the temple ("Your foundation shall be laid"). In time, against all probability, pagan kings had begun to allow the captive exiles to return to their homeland. God was fulfilling his Word. We read in 2 Chronicles 36:22, "In the first year of Cyrus king of Persia, in order to fulfill the word of the LORD spoken by Jeremiah, the LORD moved the heart of Cyrus king of Persia to make a proclamation throughout his realm and also to put it in writing" (NIV).

Remember that part, the writing. That's important.

Verse 23 continues: "This is what Cyrus king of Persia says: 'The LORD, the God of heaven, has given me all the kingdoms of the earth and he has appointed me to build a temple for him at Jerusalem in Judah. Any of his people among you may go up, and may the LORD their God be with them'" (NIV).

There are commentators who hypothesize that Cyrus was not merely showing compassion to his enslaved people by letting them go home and reestablish their own temples and worship, but he was also hedging his bets. He figured if they were all praying to their own gods for him, somebody was sure to be paying attention somewhere, and he would be in good order with some god or other.

But whatever Cyrus's motives were, God had promised through Isaiah and Jeremiah that Cyrus would be his shepherd— Isaiah actually uses that word, *shepherd*—to rebuild Jerusalem and the temple.

So here we see the first of many examples of the Word of the Lord finding its fulfillment in the mixed motives of a pagan king.

One of my favorite proverbs says that the heart of the king is like a stream of water in the hand of the Lord (Prov. 21:1). We see it here.

Back to Hanani's news to Nehemiah. This destruction of the wall and the gates is new destruction on top of old; it is destruction of the rebuilding that had commenced, sanctioned by Cyrus, king of Persia, when he began allowing the conquered people to return to their homelands and reestablish their worship and their cultures.

If we look in the book of Ezra, which is essentially a companion piece to Nehemiah, we see that the first wave of exiles had returned under the leadership of Zerubbabel, whose first priority was to rebuild the temple so that worship could recommence. The return had started and the rebuilding had begun, but then disaster had struck—the pressure of surrounding adversaries brought the work to a halt, and it was not to be resumed until about fifteen years later, when Zerubbabel's temple was finally completed with the encouragement of the prophets Haggai and Zechariah.

Again, during the return under Ezra half a century later, pressure from surrounding enemies halted the rebuilding—this time of the city and its walls. In a fast-forward section of Ezra 4, we learn that the officials of the Trans-Euphrates region reported to King Artaxerxes—that's Nehemiah's king, remember—concerning the progress in Jerusalem. Artaxerxes stopped the rebuilding of the wall lest Jerusalem become secure again and perhaps stop paying tribute and taxes. The king decided the work should stop until he had a chance to think it over and determine whether it was in his own best interest to let it continue.

This was an unmitigated disaster. It was actually worse in some ways than the original destruction and exile. The return of the exiles had been promised and had begun, but now it seemed as though God's Word, in the process of being fulfilled, had been stopped by evil men who had axes to grind and didn't want to see Jerusalem reconstituted.

Without a secure wall to defend the people from predators, raiders, and the surrounding powerful nations, there would be no permanent restoration of Israelite culture. Their heritage, their way of life, would cease. They would be assimilated into the surrounding cultures. The law and the Word of God would be forgotten as the remnant intermarried, and they all would just go away. There would be no more Israelite nation to bring forth God's promised Messiah.

So the return of the exiles and the rebuilding of Jerusalem were not just part of the normal longing for a national homeland; they were key ingredients in God's redemptive plan for the world, because the Messiah was to come out of the Israelite nation. But there wasn't an Israelite nation anymore, and there was never going to be one unless this rebuilding took place.

With the king's permission temporarily suspended, the surrounding peoples had lost no time in destroying the work that had been done on the walls. Now it looked as if the return of the exiles and the resumption of their lives as a distinct Jewish people were in jeopardy. This was Hanani's news.

Let's return to our action movie. Pan to Nehemiah's face. Something has to be done. Something *will* be done. *He* will be the one to do it. He leaps into action and . . . sits down to weep and pray to God for four months.

This is where I might lose the interest of any potential moviemaker I might have had hooked to this point.

Nehemiah leaps into action and prays for four months. In our short-attention-span world, it does not look like it, but Nehemiah is actually hard at work. We would focus on the presenting problem—the walls are broken, the gates are burned, the remnant's at risk—and come up with a plan of action, address the circumstance, and fix the problem.

Let me say, as an aside, that circumstances can often be very painful, but they are rarely our biggest problem. Our sickness, our money problems, our singleness, our marriage problems, our kids, or our infertility—these are hard, but they are not our deepest, truest needs.

Nehemiah has a much broader perspective than we typically do. He knows how God has been working in history since the creation and fall, and that the restoration of Jerusalem is but one part of the great story arc of redemption, which one day will climax with the coming of the messianic King prophesied for so many years, actually beginning with God's words to Eve in Genesis 3. So the action he takes is in light of God's Word.

The rest of what I want to say falls under two headings: (1) Nehemiah understood God's Word and (2) Nehemiah's actions were based in confidence in God's Word.

Nehemiah Understood God's Word

Follow me here. The Bible is made up of many individual stories like Nehemiah's, but in truth it is only one story: the story of God redeeming his people and restoring his world.

Some theologians break this into four parts: creation, fall, redemption, and restoration. Those are all helpful categories, but the overarching narrative is about the true Adam, the Redeemer of the world, coming to redeem a people from every tongue, tribe, and nation, and usher in the new heavens and the new earth.

The Bible is about Jesus, from before the foundation of the earth. He himself taught this truth to his disciples on the road to Emmaus: "Beginning with Moses and all the Prophets, he explained to them what was said in all the Scriptures concerning himself" (Luke 24:27 NIV). Earlier, Jesus rebuked the Pharisees by saying: "You study the Scriptures diligently because you think that in them you have eternal life. These are the very Scriptures that testify about me, yet you refuse to come to me to have life" (John 5:39–40 NIV).

The Bible is not primarily about wisdom for living, promises for comfort, or guidance for the perplexed. All those things can be found within the Bible, it's true, but they are as shiny pebbles that distract our attention from the great highway running from ruin to renewal. If we read the Scripture stories, the Psalms, the prophets, or the law disconnected from the primary narrative arc of redemption, we will find them distracting or confusing, and hard to apply properly to life today.

Unfortunately, many of us are barely literate when it comes to the flow of redemptive history. We go to our Bibles for something to help us deal with our circumstances rather than to see how God is dealing with the world. But the Bible is not about us; it's about God and his plan to redeem his fallen, miserable world, and restore it to the glory he first sang into being at creation.

Nehemiah knows there is infinitely more at stake here than just the restoration of one people's national sovereignty. He's interpreting the present problem in light of the whole Word of God. He actually alludes to this in his prayer, which we'll consider just below. (The prayer in Nehemiah 9 will more fully reveal the large scriptural perspective on the people's present situation.)

We can't read the book rightly unless we understand all of this. We know through hindsight that the promise is going to be fulfilled through an individual, a Messiah. Nehemiah's whole work is to prepare the way for him, to have a rebuilt nation, city, temple, priesthood, and sacrifices, a place where Jesus can grow up Jewish and be the true Israel, the final temple, the high priest, the ultimate sacrifice. Nehemiah doesn't precisely know how what he is doing will bring this about. But he knows he has to be faithful to God's promises and his Word.

With far less excuse than Nehemiah, many of us are a bit fuzzy on how to read our Bibles and how to find direction for our actions in light of the whole Word of God. For many of us, this is because we have been existing on a diet of artificial inspiration and devotionals rather than taking the time to sort out the Bible as a whole.

How many of you are label readers when you go grocery shopping, checking the amount of fat, sugar, salt, and preservatives in various products? Here's another question: What would be your response if you took something off the shelf and discovered the ingredients were, in this order: sugar, salt, wood ester alcohol, benzochromium hydroxate, artificial flavor, artificial color, and preservatives? I suspect that many of us would quickly place that item on the shelf next to the bug poison, back away slowly, and then run for the organic food section.

Yet we think little about feeding our souls with equally toxic, nonfood substances instead of the milk and the meat of God's Word. People can find the Word of God mysterious if not completely mystifying when they neglect the work required to unearth its meaning, so they turn to preprocessed soul junk food.

I am not saying that we have to sign up for a seminary education, although I recommend that women be as theologically educated as possible; this can only be good for the church. It can be as simple as reading Jen Wilkin's excellent book *Women of the Word*.[1]

In light of God's purpose to redeem his people from sin, as expressed through his promises to Abraham, it is clear to see that Nehemiah is not upset just because the restoration effort seems to have stalled indefinitely; he's upset because God's people are still in disgrace. That's clear from Nehemiah 1:3. God's promises look as if they have been frustrated by the designs of evil men.

Nehemiah is interpreting the present events and his own situation and gifts in light of God's Word and in light of the main themes of the Word. He doesn't need to ask for a sign, lay out a fleece, request an angelic visitor, or even read a particularly appropriate devotional, like a Christian version of a horoscope. Nehemiah understands the Word and he sees where his people are in the progression of redemptive history, so he seeks to enable them to be the people of God so the Lord will continue his plan to save the world through them.

---

[1] Jen Wilkin, *Women of the Word: How to Study the Bible with Both Our Hearts and Our Minds* (Wheaton, IL: Crossway, 2014).

Only when we can do the same thing can we read the Bible without falling into a kind of "If I do this, God will bless me" moralism. Yes, we will see lots of lessons on how to pray or how to handle worry and face opposition, but those lessons will be tied to the gospel of salvation through Christ.

The connector between Nehemiah's understanding of God's Word and his subsequent action is his prayer in chapter 1. This is the bridge between "in light of God's Word" and "taking action." Nehemiah says he prays night and day, and he mentions Kislev in the beginning and Nisan at the end (Neh. 1:1; 2:1). That indicates he is probably praying this prayer night and day for sixteen weeks. Of course, the prayer itself (1:5–11) has to be a summary of that long, long prayer time, but it shows the trajectory of his weeks of prayer.

First, in verse 5, Nehemiah spends time just looking at God: he is heavenly, great, awesome. And while, yes, he keeps his covenant of love, it's with those who love him and obey his commands. Nehemiah begins in a remarkably God-centered way, recognizing God's complete freedom. He actually owes us nothing. Derek Kidner says Nehemiah begins by putting us in our place.[2]

That's not the way we modern people usually pray, is it? We start with our own feelings or needs. Or if we start with God, we want to hear warm, fuzzy reassurances from him, speaking to our hearts. Nehemiah, it seems, starts by getting his heart reoriented. Even the most godly people tend to lose perspective under the stress of a crisis, and Nehemiah doesn't want to let that happen to him.

When we don't realize how infinitely great God is, all kinds of distortions creep into our thinking. We panic or obsess because we forget that our God is infinitely great. Ironically, admitting he owes us nothing and that he is majestic, high, and lofty brings more peace than lots of crying out with desperate petitions.

[2] Derek Kidner, *Ezra and Nehemiah: An Introduction & Commentary*, Tyndale Old Testament Commentaries (Downers Grove, IL: InterVarsity Press, 1979), 79.

After adoration comes confession (vv. 6–7). This, too, comes before any petition. In this, Nehemiah is actually following the model that Jesus put into the Lord's Prayer. Nehemiah confesses both his individual sin and the corporate sin of his people. According to Kidner, after adoring God's infinite highness and confessing our smallness, we realize God owes us nothing, and therefore we come empty-handed.[3] That's the only way we can come into his presence. There's no way we can put a claim on God.

Finally, Nehemiah makes his appeal to God (vv. 8–10). He does so based firmly on God's own Word. He references Deuteronomy, which affirms that God has promised to bring his people back from exile and reconstitute a nation and a house, Jerusalem and the temple, where God's name will dwell (12:5; 30:4). He alludes to Exodus in verse 10, reminding God how he redeemed his people from Egypt by his mighty hand. God has gone to a lot of trouble already to create this people, and now they need him to fulfill his promises in order to continue as a people.

There had been times when the nation of Israel had sinned so badly as to be on the verge of extinction and final abandonment by God. But Moses had interceded in prayer, and God's work with Israel had gone forward. Now Nehemiah is interceding in the same way. Again we see Nehemiah's prayer grounded in the Word, in the history of salvation, and in the conviction that God will fulfill his promises and continue his work of redemption.

So the first action Nehemiah takes (our title, remember, is "Taking Action in Light of God's Word") is prayer. Similarly, our prayers should always be in light of the Word. Our prayer life should be shaped and grounded in Scripture as often as possible, as we respond to scriptural promises and statements about God.

Immersion in God's Word teaches us to pray the same way immersion in language teaches a baby how to speak the language of her parents. Praying Scripture-filled prayers radically reorients

---

[3] Ibid.

us away from our self-absorption, giving us perspective, removing our worry and our panic, by humbling us before God.

Nehemiah Had Confidence in God's Word

Nehemiah also takes action based on confidence in God's Word. At the end of chapter 1, he reveals two important pieces of information that will shape the course of action he's planning to take after praying.

Nehemiah asks for God's favor with "this man" (v. 11), who in the next sentence is revealed as Nehemiah's employer, none other than King Artaxerxes. As cupbearer to the king, Nehemiah has the trust and the access to Artaxerxes that very few others have. He decides to risk that position and possibly his life to ask for a huge personal favor. He's going to go to the king directly, using his position as cupbearer to get access, and make a request. He knows the danger, and he approaches it in a very humble, vulnerable way.

Verse 11 is striking; despite how slowly Nehemiah gets there—four months of praying, adoration, confession, all of it—when he gets there, he has a very specific plan and a very specific request worked out. The king could be furious. In fact, Nehemiah says, "I was very much afraid" (2:2). Nehemiah knows there is a lot on the line. This is the king who stopped the work of rebuilding and allowed the marauders to destroy the half-built wall. Now Nehemiah is going to ask him to reverse that decision.

I want to pause here to consider the sovereignty of God at work behind the scenes. We can go back in the book of Ezra and see events that had been unfolding at the highest level of red tape. Letters concerning the legality of the wall rebuilding had flown back and forth at the speed of camel between Jerusalem and Artaxerxes's citadel at Susa. To begin with, we are told in Ezra 4 that Rehum and Shimshai wrote Artaxerxes, accusing the Jews of rebuilding Jerusalem with a view of seceding from the empire and escaping the taxes and revenues due it (vv. 9–16). Artaxerxes responded with his own letter, the order to stop work until he could think it over (vv. 17–22). Providentially, he allowed for the issuance of another decree changing his mind (v. 21).

Ezra tells of this halting of work in his and Nehemiah's time (4:7–23) in the context of telling about the similar halting back in Zerubbabel's time (4:1–5 and 4:24–6:22). So this persecution is nothing new! But God has sovereignly directed. Under Zerubbabel took place one of the most celebrated victories of clerks and paper pushers everywhere and a shining example of God working behind the scenes through bureaucratic red tape. At that time, enemies also sent letters to the king, then Darius. The governors of the Trans-Euphrates—everything past the Euphrates River—and the little potentates of that region wrote to Darius and tattled that the Jews were rebuilding without permission and were defending their actions by saying first that God had told them to and second that King Cyrus had given them permission in the past and had even returned the gold and silver articles that had been looted from the temple. These tattlers asked for a search of the royal archives of Babylon to see if this so-called decree of Cyrus could be found, and also asked for an answer.

Do you remember that I told you it was important that Cyrus had written his decree down?

King Darius issued the order, the archival search proceeded, and a memorandum was found (Ezra 6:2), a divinely filed memorandum showing that Cyrus had indeed issued a decree not merely *permitting* but *ordering* the rebuilding of Jerusalem. Darius conveyed this information to the governors, together with the surely unwelcome orders to assist the rebuilding with whatever was needed: money, animals for sacrifice, and anything else requested by the priests in Jerusalem. Anyone ignoring this order would be impaled on a beam taken from his own house. The rest of Ezra 6 describes the joyful completion of the temple rebuilding under Zerubbabel.

Be careful what you ask for when you ask for a search of the royal archives.

The providence and omnipotence of God have been protecting his people through every stage of this painful process of returning and rebuilding. Nehemiah knows this. He knows God's faithfulness in the past, and he's basing his present actions on knowing that God will not stop being faithful to the word he's spoken to bring the exiles back and to rebuild their city. Like his contemporary Esther, he has risen to his position for just such a time as this.

Nehemiah shows the king great deference: "Let the king live forever!" (Neh. 2:3). Then, when the king asks what Nehemiah wants from him, Nehemiah makes his famous brief "arrow prayer," his inward prayer (v. 4), and essentially goes for broke. If God is going to show him favor, if God is going to continue to fulfill his promise to bring the exiles back to their land and their heritage, it will be now.

First, Nehemiah asks to be allowed to return personally to Jerusalem. He asks for permission to rebuild it (v. 5). Then he goes further and asks for letters giving the royal seal of approval to his mission so he'll have safe passage (v. 7). Oh, and one more thing: he asks for carte blanche to access the timber in the royal forest for the building project (v. 8).

The king says yes to everything, and even sends army officers and cavalry soldiers with Nehemiah on his journey back to Jerusalem (vv. 8–9), possibly as a token of his approval of the project and no doubt also for protection from hostile forces.

Convinced that God has given him the king's favor for which he prayed, Nehemiah just keeps asking. It reminds me of that line in John Newton's hymn: "Thou art coming to a King; large petitions with thee bring."[4] Newton is actually talking about prayer to God, but Nehemiah gets the principle.

Nehemiah demonstrates, in an almost outlandish way, his confidence in God's Word. If you're going to ask in line with God's glory and to further God's redemptive purposes, ask big—and

4 From the hymn "Come, My Soul, Thy Suit Prepare" by John Newton, 1779.

look for help God may send through all kinds of sources. That's what Nehemiah does, and the king, for motives known only to himself, becomes Nehemiah's patron, supplying him with whatever he needs to accomplish the task that God has given him.

The book *Gospel Patrons*, by John Rinehart, contains stories of modern-day men and women of generosity who have supported gospel-led people and movements.[5] While they're not the faces of such movements, these patrons are the givers who make them move. In like manner, King Artaxerxes doesn't lift a finger personally to rebuild Jerusalem, but without his patronage, Nehemiah cannot do what God has called him to do. Kings' hearts, and all patrons' hearts, are in God's hand.

Nehemiah's journey to Jerusalem is recorded with four words: "I went to Jerusalem" (v. 11). It is another action taken on full trust and confidence in God's Word. He leaves the world he has known, the privilege and security of the palace. He heads into unknown opposition. There's no mention of the thousand-mile journey on camel, horse, or foot, with heat, sand, flies, discomfort, and danger of all sorts. No. Just "I went to Jerusalem." The rest is sort of beside the point.

Once in Jerusalem, Nehemiah allows himself three days of rest and recovery, then sets out to reconnoiter the damage (vv. 11–16). He goes on a secret overnight survey to inspect the walls from the outside, looking for any weaknesses that would be apparent to the enemy. Does he stop to ask, "What do I, a cupbearer to the king, know about defensible walls or building codes?" No—action must be taken, so he takes the action.

This is a tangent, but I really want you to remember this. Often, God calls you to a ministry by making you the one who sees the need that others don't. Rather than haranguing your pastor, your elders, or the person in the seat next to you about why they don't have a ministry to the elderly, why the church is not doing vaca-

---

[5] John Rinehart, *Gospel Patrons* (Fullerton, CA: Reclaimed Publishing, 2014).

tion Bible school in that needy neighborhood over there, or why they don't have this or that support for married couples, realize that perhaps you are seeing the need because God is calling you to be the one who meets the need, the one who starts the ministry or just starts doing it yourself.

This is something I've observed many, many times in our forty years in the ministry: somebody will be really agitated and asking why the church isn't doing this or that. I say, "Well, you're seeing it, and you're agitated because God has given you the ministry to do something about it." So the next time you have a burr under your saddle blanket about something, just consider that it might be God who put it there.

When Nehemiah finally speaks to the remnant living in Jerusalem, comprised of priests, nobles, officials, and the ordinary people who will actually do the work, he gets them on board by recounting how God's hand has been with him up till then, including the interview with the king and its abundant outcome (vv. 17–20). Referring to the disgrace of Jerusalem's brokenness, he again uses language referring to God's redemptive purposes. He locates their situation in redemptive history, not just the immediate need. They have been disgraced, exiled, and humbled because of their sin. But now God's promise to restore Israel as a nation is coming to fruition. And who wouldn't want to be a part of that? God's Word is in the process of being fulfilled. Don't you want to get in on the action?

The Whole Main Point

In just these first two chapters, Nehemiah has abundantly shown us on many occasions how he has taken radical action based on his knowledge of God's Word and redemptive promises. We have a lot to learn from him: his knowledge of the Word of God that undergirded him, and how he trusted and acted in light of that Word.

But that's not the whole main message.

The biggest message of Nehemiah is that it's not about Nehemiah. All of Scripture tells about who? Jesus. I've heard Nehemiah preached as someone who changed careers because he was pursuing his passion; as a person who left the big company for a small start-up because he was doing what he loved; and even as a social activist trying to help the oppressed. All of that is plausible, but none of it's accurate.

Because of his understanding of the Word of God and God's plan to bless all the nations through Israel, Nehemiah determined that he should leave his secure place in the palace at the right hand of the king and go out into a dangerous situation, where the chances not just of failure but of persecution and assassination were high. He was driven by his understanding of God's promises and his redemptive plan.

If we don't understand this ourselves, then when we read the Bible, perhaps we'll take away a list of wise principles of leadership to apply in situations that seem vaguely familiar. Are we in the midst of a building campaign to repair the church? Preach on Nehemiah. Are we experiencing opposition to God's purposes in the world? Think about how Nehemiah handled opposition.

I'm not deriding these principles. Some of them have great usefulness. In fact, I'll call out two of them that I mentioned in passing.

First, I noted that Nehemiah inspected the broken wall from the outside, from his enemy's vantage point—in order to understand what his enemies would see as weaknesses. So, too, we are always to try to understand the point of view of people who differ from us and to see what they see when they look at us in order to shore up our apologetic weaknesses and learn to speak in language that skeptics and unbelievers can understand. That's a good lesson.

Second, when Ezra went to Jerusalem (see Ezra 8:22), he specifically decided *not* to ask the king for soldiers and horsemen to protect him on the journey. His reasoning was that after claiming God's power to protect him, he would be ashamed to ask for human protection, as if he doubted God's power or willingness to watch over him. Ezra and his group even fasted and prayed about making this decision, and, convinced it was the right one, Ezra entrusted twelve priests and ten of their brothers with a fortune of gold and silver to be used in the temple. They set out on that dangerous thousand-mile journey with no escort from the king.

But when Nehemiah goes on the same journey thirteen years later, he gratefully accepts an armed escort as evidence that God is the one behind the king's favor. He has not made similar claims about God's protection that might seem to be contradicted by asking for human protection. And, to be sure, he remembers that it was Artaxerxes himself who had earlier stopped the wall building when opponents had craftily sent their petition; how important it is, then, to bring Artaxerxes on board with this project, helping him become heavily invested in it and thereby surely less likely to be turned against it again. These were two different decisions by two different godly men in two different historical circumstances.

Commentator Raymond Brown has this to say about the differing choices of Ezra and Nehemiah:

> One man's commitment to God precluded the escort; the other welcomed it. Ezra regarded soldiers as a lack of confidence in God's power; Nehemiah viewed them as evidence of God's superlative goodness.
>
> Christians frequently differ on important issues, and it's a mark of spiritual maturity if they can handle those differences creatively rather than engaging in damaging verbal warfare. First-century believers differed on some questions, and Paul urged them to "stop passing judgment on one another." . . .
>
> We are bound to think differently on occasions. Before we hastily judge other believers or ostracize them, we must make every attempt to understand and love them, and discern what we can learn from them as we "make every effort to do what leads to peace and mutual edification" (Rom. 14:19).

We must not rigidly stereotype believers into identical patterns of spirituality.[6]

Those final words of Brown's are important. Ezra and Nehemiah came to totally different conclusions. They reasoned, fasted, and prayed, but they came up with different answers, two opposite strategies for glorifying God, both of which were right. God sometimes asks people to act in different ways. Let's be charitable with one another.

We should examine our hearts to see where we have baptized our own preferences or our cultural differences while labeling any other practices as less honoring to God. God may have different plans for different people in different situations.

But as helpful and useful as these and other applications may be, they're not the point of Nehemiah. "All the Scriptures tell of me," Jesus said (see John 5:39). Not only was Nehemiah playing his role in redemptive history by seeing that the Israelites were reconstituted as a people according to God's promise so as to bring forth the shoot from the stump of Jesse, Jesus, David's greater son—Nehemiah himself was acting out the career of Christ.

There's an old-timey hymn we used to sing at the church where Tim served years ago in Hopewell, Virginia. The refrain begins with these words: "Out of the ivory palaces, into a world of woe."[7] Nehemiah literally left a palace and went to a broken world of woe where God's people were in need. He left privilege and safety for hardship and back-breaking labor. If he hadn't done it, Jerusalem would not have been rebuilt, and there would have been no Jewish culture for Jesus to be raised in, and therefore no Jewish Messiah to fulfill God's promises.

Nehemiah was God's instrument in a critical moment of redemptive history, but his story is submerged in the greater story. Jesus is the greater Nehemiah, the one who left the heavenly pal-

---

[6] Raymond Brown, *The Message of Nehemiah: God's Servant in a Time of Change*, The Bible Speaks Today commentary series (Downers Grove, IL: InterVarsity Press, 1998), 50.
[7] From the hymn "Ivory Palaces" by Henry Barraclough, 1915.

ace, the right hand of the King, safety, and glory to come into a world of need. He joined the blue-collar labor force as a carpenter, and spent most of his thirty-three years building things. He came not just at the risk of death, but with the certainty of it. But if Jesus had not done it, our salvation would not have been accomplished.

In Nehemiah, we see an ordinary man serving under the oppression, however benevolent, of a foreign power. What Nehemiah sees is his country in tatters, a shadow of its former glory under Moses, David, and Solomon, self-destroyed and at its lowest point. He and others scrape together a small remnant that sets itself apart, resumes God-designed worship and a godly lifestyle, and carries on, however heartbreakingly reduced in power and glory, the life of the covenant people of God. But it is enough.

God's people do not need to be powerful culturally or in power politically to be obedient to him and accomplish his purposes in the world. All they need to do to glorify him and join the great sweep of redemptive history is to be faithful to the One who has called them by his own name.

Let us not do less than Nehemiah, because we are called by the One who is greater than Nehemiah, and he will accomplish it.

Reflect and Pray

Reflect on each question, and then take a moment to speak or write the prayers that grow from those reflections.

1. Kathy Keller starts by placing the book of Nehemiah in the flow of Old Testament history. Read 2 Chronicles 36:15–23 to review the background of Ezra and Nehemiah. What phrases show what God is like and how he is involved in this story of his people?
2. Find and reflect on the references to "hand" and "hands" in Nehemiah 1–2. What truths does the narrator want to be sure to emphasize?
3. Kathy's chapter emphasizes Nehemiah's trust in God's Word—ultimately in God's promises to bless Nehemiah's

people and, through their seed, to bless all the nations. That trust shaped his action. How does God's grace in the life of this ordinary man personally challenge you to take action today in light of God's Word?

Think Like an Expositor

Kathy Keller had the huge, challenging job of helping us dive into this Old Testament narrative. Her comparison of the plot with an action movie shows one of the delights of this genre: the stories are really good! Old Testament narratives abound with vivid characters and action that draw us in. Nehemiah, the first-person narrator, is quite a masterful storyteller—as well as a good leader of his people.

This talk helpfully acknowledged some of the tensions of meeting such an admirable character as Nehemiah and being tempted to spend all one's time drawing out moral lessons from his behavior. Even though there are a lot of good things to learn, we were carefully pointed here to the story's context—first, the complex historical context, with several waves of returning Jewish exiles ruled by Persians who had conquered the Babylonians who had conquered Jerusalem and taken its people captive. We also were led to grasp the larger biblical context, the context of God's promises that through this remnant of a people would come the seed of blessing, the eternal King. The largest lessons of this talk were not just about trusting God's Word, but about Jesus, who shines through this Word.

When we asked Kathy how she worked on this talk, she responded with three brief points, the first of which was that the task of exposition is hard. She said she struggled, having spoken many times topically but not many times expositionally. Many will be able to identify with this struggle.

Her third point delineated her process of study, which is also encouraging, as she mentioned the basics: reading, underlining, taking notes, using commentaries and sticky notes, putting the text away for a while and then coming back to search for more, trying to think of an introduction, seeing how the passage is about Jesus—the list is a great reminder of the process of work involved in digging into a text.

Kathy had a bit of an unfair advantage, though. Point no. 2, in the center of her list: "I have listened to Tim's preaching for 40 years, so I used his preaching as my model." Actually, how wonderful is that!

2

Laboring for a God Who Fights for Us

Nehemiah 3-4

Tim Keller

We are studying Nehemiah not only to learn from the book itself but also to learn *how to learn* from the book. Some of the Old Testament books—such as Nehemiah and Esther—are difficult to study because they show the weakness in our approach to Scripture.

For example, when we read the book of Nehemiah as Christians today, this is what we see: the Jews came back from Babylon and had to rebuild the wall of Jerusalem. They faced tremendous opposition. Nonetheless, they stayed with it. They organized well. They prayed. They asked God *not* to forgive their enemies (did I read that right?). In the end, they persevered and got the wall built.

Now, how do we apply that to our lives? The answer seems to have to do with leadership and organizational principles. The third chapter, for example, is often said to teach delegation. If you have a big job to do, divide it into parts and delegate them to others. The fourth chapter then teaches how to solve problems—how to overcome opposition and so forth.

But this answer shows the shallowness of our approach to Scripture. It shows that we tend to come to the Bible the way we come to *Aesop's Fables*. We read a story and then identify the moral of that story. So, when we read about David and Goliath, we see that the moral of the story is "The bigger they come, the harder they fall." When we read Nehemiah, we get leadership principles. Well, obviously, it is true that the bigger they come, the harder they fall. And it is true we can get leadership principles out of Nehemiah. Yet certainly neither "moral" gets to the heart of the matter.

Studying a book like Nehemiah forces us to go back to what we understand the Bible to be. I'd like to show you two basic parts to the doctrine of Scripture. The Bible, on the one hand, is a human book, which means we don't believe—as did Joseph Smith about *The Book of Mormon*—that it was written on golden plates by angels or by God himself. It was written by human beings who used Greek, Aramaic, or Hebrew words. Therefore, we need to understand what those words meant and how those languages worked, because human beings used them to give us the message.

On the other hand, the Bible is a divine book. It was written by God; every word on the page is there because God guided the human author to write that word. That means the Bible is ultimately one story. It is one large story comprised of many little stories. There's one large narrative arc, and everything in the Bible is moving and pointing along that arc.

The Ultimate Nehemiah and the Ultimate City

It is in this context that we come to Nehemiah. We know that this Nehemiah is pointing to the ultimate Nehemiah—the ultimate One who was in the palace, completely safe, and left all of that to go out into danger to identify with his people. Jesus Christ, the ultimate Nehemiah, identified with us—not at the *risk* of his life but at the *cost* of his life—to make us citizens of the ultimate city.

We see this trajectory throughout the Bible. In Isaiah 26:1–2, Isaiah is looking forward to the city of God and says, "We have a strong city." Right away, we think of Jerusalem. But then he says: "[God] sets up salvation as walls and bulwarks. Open the gates, that the righteous nation that keeps faith may enter in." Even in the Old Testament, Jerusalem is a sign of something bigger that is yet to come. Not literal walls, but walls of salvation are going to protect us from sin and death itself. Not a physical city, but a spiritual city will come down out of heaven at the end of time and turn the heavens and earth into the new heavens and earth. So it is only when we put Nehemiah—or whatever part of the Bible we are reading—into that larger story and begin to see it pointing along the greater narrative arc that Scripture really begins to open up.

There is a certain sense in which we can't directly apply Nehemiah to ourselves today. Is it right for the people of God to build a wall around themselves to keep out all the unbelievers—to be physically and culturally isolated? Is it right to call down curses on our enemies or to say to God, "Please don't forgive them"? No, it isn't.

Nehemiah was operating at a different stage in redemptive history, a point when God was bringing his salvation through people who existed as a nation-state—and a nation-state could not exist without a capital city with a wall around it. The wall provided the security needed for urban life to develop, creating a place for jurisprudence, commerce, and stable social structures. So Nehemiah is not just following his passion. He's not just practicing good leadership and organizational skills to create economic prosperity for his particular people group. He knows that if God is to continue to do his work as the covenant God, the people have to be faithful to him. They have to be covenant people—not just a nation-state with a capital city, but God's chosen people, with Jerusalem as the city of God where they worship in the temple and trace the promises of a king in David's line. In that stage of redemptive history, this is how God worked.

We also have to build up the people of God, but we do it differently today. We also need a wall around us, in a sense, so that we are helping people be holy and separate, but we do that by sanctification through the means of grace. They were building a temporary city with a physical wall; we are building the ultimate eternal city through conversion. That is what the New Testament tells us. We are making people citizens of that city through the gospel of Jesus Christ, and we are building that city when we do the work of the church. When we begin to see the larger narrative arc and where the particular story fits in that narrative, then things start to open up.

With that in mind, we now turn to the third and fourth chapters of the book of Nehemiah.

One Whole Holy City

It's interesting to me that probably the most popular best-selling Christian book on the book of Nehemiah in the last twenty to thirty years is Chuck Swindoll's *Hand Me Another Brick*. He does not even cover chapter 3 in that book. I think you will understand why as you look at the chapter; it's long and feels tedious in places. And yet, the whole thing is precious. I love this chapter now that I understand what it is pointing to and where it fits in redemptive history.

What is extraordinarily impressive in this chapter, especially if you read it carefully, is that both men and women are working. You have both clergy and laity working. You have groups from different towns. You have groups from different classes. You have groups from different trades. You have rulers and workers, goldsmiths and merchants and perfumers. You have representatives from virtually every part of society, and you have one phrase repeated over and over throughout the text: "next to him" (or "them").

Most scholars have noticed that this inclusiveness is part of a progression in the Bible, from God's working primarily through prominent individuals, such as Moses and David, to his working instead through the whole people of God. When you read the story of Moses, for example, it feels as if he is carrying the entire nation of Israel on his back. Time after time, the people go astray. They quickly forget God's commands and even more quickly forget their own promises to obey. Time after time, God says: "Stand aside, Moses. I am going to take them out." And time after time, Moses puts himself between the people and God, as it were, and says: "No, don't do that. Take me out instead."

When we come to Nehemiah, we see something different. Here is a task that the clergy cannot do by themselves. The clergy are working right next to everybody else. Everyone is participating. Everyone is doing the work. There has been a movement away from the ministry being done by just one or two leaders to it being done by the whole people of God. Rebuilding the people of God is the work of the whole people of God. Everybody has to do it.

What this means is pretty simple. It's pointing toward the fact that there is a progression in the history of redemption when it comes to holiness. The priests dedicated the wall—the Hebrew word is *qadash*—which means they pronounced it holy (Neh. 3:1). The priests pronounced it holy, but the whole people built it.

We see this progression in the history of redemption as we move through the Bible. In the earliest parts, God comes down temporarily. God appears to Jacob in his dream of the stairway, and when Jacob awakes, he names the place "Bethel," saying, "This is . . . the house of God" (Gen. 28:10–17). It is, and yet it isn't. God appeared there. His holy presence was there, but now it is gone. Bethel is not actually the house of God because it is not a place where God's presence resides in a sustained way.

Later, we see the tabernacle and the temple. Now God's holiness dwells in a place. It dwells in the Holy of Holies, where the Shekinah glory cloud is over the ark of the covenant. God's actual presence, in a sense, resides in a fixed way in the midst of his people.

In the book of Isaiah, there is a fascinating prophecy about the future:

> In that day the Branch of the LORD will be beautiful and glorious, and the fruit of the land will be the pride and glory of the survivors in Israel. Those who are left in Zion, who remain in Jerusalem, will be called holy, all who are recorded among the living in Jerusalem. The Lord will wash away the filth of the women of Zion; he will cleanse the bloodstains from Jerusalem by a spirit of judgment and a spirit of fire. Then the LORD will create over all of Mount Zion and over those who assemble there a cloud of smoke by day and a glow of flaming fire by night; over everything the glory will be a canopy. It will be a shelter and shade from the heat of the day, and a refuge and hiding place from the storm and rain. (4:2–6 NIV)

This is astounding. We are told here about a time when the holiness of God—his Shekinah glory—will not be in a temple in the midst of the people, but rather over the *whole* people. It will be a day when all the people will be holy, a day when the glory of God will dwell in a group of people, not just in a building.

Then again, at the climax of the book of Zechariah, we read this:

> On that day HOLY TO THE LORD will be inscribed on the bells of the horses, and the cooking pots in the LORD's house will be like the sacred bowls in front of the altar. Every pot in Jerusalem and Judah will be holy to the LORD Almighty, and all who come to sacrifice will take some of the pots and cook in them. And on that day there will no longer be a Canaanite in the house of the LORD Almighty. (14:20–21 NIV)

In Zechariah's time, if a pot or utensil was to be used only for the Lord's work, it was inscribed "Holy to the Lord" and was put in the tabernacle or the temple. But on "that day," even the bridles on the horses, even the pots in the kitchen, will say, "Holy to the Lord."

Someday, the holiness of God, the glory of God, will break out of the building, as it were, and all the people will be holy—a living temple. The whole city and everyone in it will be holy. It won't be just ethnic Jews, but every race in the city will be holy. There will no longer be a Canaanite in the house of God because they won't be called Canaanites anymore. Isaiah tells us that someday God will call Egypt "my people" and Assyria "my handiwork" (Isa. 19:25).

What are all these things looking toward? Most scholars believe that when, here in the book of Nehemiah, not just the temple but the whole city is called holy (11:1, 18)—with all the people working together—it is pointing in the direction of when Jesus Christ died on the cross and the veil in the temple was torn from top to bottom (Matt. 27:50–51). Ephesians 2 and 1 Peter 2 say that we now are living stones being built together into a living temple. We have the Holy Spirit in us. The very thing that was once in the tabernacle is now somehow in us. Moses said, "Lord, show me Your glory," and God said, "No, it would destroy you" (see Ex. 33:18–20); yet the apostle John says, "The Word became flesh and dwelt [literally "tabernacled"] among us, and we have seen his glory, glory as of the only Son from the Father, full of grace and truth" (John 1:14). And again, 2 Corinthians talks about our "beholding the glory of the Lord . . . in the face of Jesus Christ" (3:18; 4:6).

Now, what does this mean? I do not exactly know what was literally happening in Nehemiah's day, but we do know that Nehemiah is pointing toward the future, when we are all prophets, priests, kings—a day when we all have the Holy Spirit—and this means two things. First, every Christian has a ministry, and, second, together we are one united whole.

A City Full of Ministers

First, we are all ministers, every single one of us. Just as Jerusalem could not be rebuilt with only the work of the clergy but required the work of all the people, so Paul says over and over that every person has gifts. Everybody is different, and we need every person. We need every gift. We are the living stones being built into the temple of God, and there are no superfluous stones.

If God in his providence has drawn you together with a hundred people to be a church, then you are not there by accident. You have a gift that is needed. You have certain people whom you can speak to. You have certain hands you can hold because of your past experiences. You have certain hearts you can reach. There are certain people to whom you can be a prophet, a priest, and a king. There are certain ways you can build up the people of God, and you would not be there unless God wants to use your gift in that community. Unless all the gifts are used, the community cannot do the work God has given it to do.

The strength of this truth comes to me especially where Jesus says an amazing thing in Matthew 11:11: "Among those born of women"—which is pretty much everybody, isn't it?—"there has not risen anyone greater than John the Baptist; yet whoever is least in the kingdom of heaven is greater than he" (NIV). I, and many commentators, have long wrestled with what this means, but it certainly seems to me to mean this: because the simplest Christian understands the gospel in a way that John the Baptist did not, because the simplest Christian has the Holy Spirit in a way that John the Baptist did not, because we live in a new stage of redemptive history when the veil has been ripped and we are the living temple—because of all these things, every single Christian today has capabilities of ministry that John the Baptist didn't have. Isn't that astounding?

Years ago, in seminary, I read a book by Michael Green called *Evangelism in the Early Church*. It was a tremendous paradigm-buster for me because he brought out a pretty simple fact that I should have already considered. He pointed out that the earliest church grew through evangelism, but he asked how that evangelism happened. It would be tempting to say that there were great preachers in those days, and, if you were a Christian, you brought your non-Christian friends to hear the great preachers. Now there is no doubt that preaching was important, especially the kind of itinerant preaching Paul did, for example. But Green points out that it was dangerous to bring non-Christians to church because in many places you might all be dead the next day if someone brought the wrong non-Christian to church. So, how did you evangelize people? *Everybody evangelized people.* You did not rely on the great preachers. You did it yourself. Every single person in the body of Christ was necessary to do the work of ministry. The ministry of the people of God required all the people of God.

A City with One People

The second thing to notice here is the unity of the people. "Next to him . . . next to him . . . next to him . . ." The commentators go into all the names and explain who they are. There are men and women, ruling class and working class, merchants and clergy, all working together. This is a foretaste and a pointer to the fact that because we are holy, we are one. We are all one in Christ.

David Martyn Lloyd-Jones, in his exposition of Ephesians, looks at the place where Paul says, "For this reason, because I have heard of your faith in the Lord Jesus and your love toward all the saints, I do not cease to give thanks for you" (1:15–16a). In his exposition of this passage, Lloyd-Jones notes that Paul gives two evidences that the Ephesians are real Christians—they have faith in Christ and they love all the saints.[1]

One of the things that is interesting about Lloyd-Jones's testimony is that he was a royal physician when he became a Christian; he worked for Lord Horder, the physician to the royal family. If he had stayed in that prominent role, he likely would have taken Lord Horder's position, which means he would have been in the House of Lords. Here is a young, brilliant Welshman who went to

---

[1] D. M. Lloyd-Jones, "The Tests of Christian Profession," in *God's Ultimate Purpose: An Exposition of Ephesians 1:1 to 23* (Grand Rapids, MI: Baker, 1979), 312–25.

medical school, became a doctor, and was on his way to the top. As a non-aristocrat, you could not have had a better career path than Lloyd-Jones did in the mid-1920s.

However, when Lloyd-Jones became a Christian, he decided he was called to the ministry. He left his incredibly promising medical career and took a little church in a poor fishing village in Wales. He was still a fairly young Christian, and he wrestled with doubts about his faith, saying that Satan would accuse him: "Very often Satan would come and suggest, 'How do you know you're a Christian?'" He didn't know what to say. But one day, after he had spent some time in Wales as a pastor in his little village, he turned around and said: "I want to know, Satan, why would I rather talk about Jesus with the humblest fisher woman in Wales? Why would I love doing that more than I love talking about medicine with my peers and other men who have gone to the same schools as me and are of the same social class?" Once he began saying that to Satan, the Devil didn't know what to reply and left him alone.[2]

Those who are not British must remember that Britain is a class-driven society compared to America, even today. In those days, it was very class-stratified, and when he went to that small Welsh village, Lloyd-Jones was hanging out with people five or six rungs below him on the social and educational ladder. But he suddenly realized that he had more in common with the humblest fisherwoman in his church in Wales than he did with people of his own status and education. He felt a bond with her, a bond with people very unlike him, that he did not feel with people who were like him racially, emotionally, socially, or educationally.

Identity has layers. My maternal grandfather was an Italian immigrant. I never met him. He died before I was born, but I understand that he was quite proud of being Italian. He loved being Italian. It was a major part of his identity. He did a lot of things—he was a butcher, a mushroom farmer, a pipefitter—but

---

[2] Ibid., 322–23.

his job just wasn't that important to him. It wasn't as foundational to his identity as his national background. However, his children were very different. My mother, for example, grew up in America and went to nursing school, and she was, in a very warranted way, quite proud of being a nurse, of being a professional. For her, being a professionally trained nurse was much more important to her identity than her Italian heritage. In other words, the layers of their identities were ordered differently.

For all of us, some things are closer to the foundation of our identity and some things are just a part of it. You might say, "Yes, of course, I'm Italian, but it's not as important as the fact that I'm a lawyer or a doctor or something like that." At the bottom of every person's heart there is an uttermost foundation. At the beginning of *The Two Towers*, the second *Lord of the Rings* movie, Gandalf battles the Balrog while they plummet down an incredible chasm—down, down, down, into the depths of the earth. The name of that place, in J. R. R. Tolkien's terminology, is "the uttermost foundations of stone." The uttermost foundations of stone is the bedrock, the bottom. You can't go any farther down. Everybody's heart, everybody's identity, has an uttermost foundation.

When you become a Christian, your conviction of sin and your experience of grace go all the way to the bottom—all the way to that uttermost foundation. Christ goes there, and no matter what happens, that foundation doesn't change. If you're Chinese and you become a Christian, you don't become an African Christian. You don't become a European Christian. You're a Chinese Christian. But your Christianity goes underneath your Chineseness. Likewise, it goes underneath your Italianness. It goes underneath your being a nurse or a lawyer. It goes underneath being an abused child. It goes underneath anything. It goes to the uttermost foundations.

Then, when you meet someone who has that same foundation—even though he or she is of a different race, a different class, a different education—you feel the bond. You say: "As different as you are, you are more my brother. You are more my sister. I feel a bond with you, a bond that I don't have with people who don't have Christ, even though they are of my same ethnicity, same class, or same education."

"Next to him . . . next to him . . . next to him . . ." All these different people—people who otherwise wouldn't have worked together on anything—now are all together. In Christ, we are holy. In Christ, we all have gifts. In Christ, we are being built together into the temple.

A City Full of Prayer and Guards

Now, as we move on to Nehemiah 4, there are two other things to tell you about. First, this is an interesting and important instance of one of the main themes of the Bible that, again, comes to a conclusion on the cross—the relationship between God's sovereignty and human responsibility. Notice that verse 9 says, "We prayed to our God and posted a guard" (NIV). Similarly, in Isaiah, there is an interesting place where Hezekiah the king knows he is about to die. He prays to the Lord to save him. God says to Hezekiah through Isaiah, "I have heard your prayer . . . I will add fifteen years to your life" (38:5 NIV). Then Isaiah adds this, "Let them take a cake of figs and apply it to the boil, that he may recover" (v. 21). It is the same thing in both cases. I prayed to God, and God said: "I will heal you. Here, take your medicine." I prayed to God, and God said: "I will deliver you. Here, take your weapon and post a guard."

Over and over again in the Bible, we see this emphasis on God's sovereignty and human responsibility as two things that go together. We have a tendency to say that if God is really protecting you, you don't have to post a guard. And if you post a guard, then you don't really believe God is protecting you. But that's not right. My favorite example of this is in Acts 27. Paul is in a boat as a prisoner on his way to Rome, so both the sailors manning the boat and the soldiers escorting him are there with him. A terrible storm comes up and rages for days. At one point, an angel of the Lord appears to Paul and tells him that no one sailing with him will die. So Paul tells everyone about it, saying, "There will be no loss of life among you, but only of the ship" (v. 22).

Now, considering how well Paul knows his Bible, this means that he is absolutely certain that nobody is going to die. Deuteronomy 18:20 says that if a prophet gives a prediction that doesn't come true, he is to be killed. He is not speaking from the Lord. First Samuel 15:29 says God "is not a man, that he should change his mind" (NIV 1984). So if God tells a prophet something is going to happen, it is going to happen. And yet, just a few verses later, despite Paul's prophecy, the sailors get worried, sneak over to the lifeboat, and start to lower it into the water. Paul finds out about it, runs to the soldiers, and says, "Unless these men stay in the ship, you cannot be saved" (Acts 27:31). Wait a minute. Why doesn't Paul say: "Hey, you know, God has promised that nobody is going to die, so it doesn't matter what you do. Take the lifeboat. Don't take the lifeboat. Go snorkeling if you want. Who cares?" No. He says, "We've all got to stay in the ship." What's going on here?

Both J. I. Packer, in his book *Evangelism and the Sovereignty of God*, and Don Carson, in his book *Divine Sovereignty and Human Responsibility*, tackle this question. If you read those books, you get a grip on something that comes together in the cross. After the crucifixion, when Peter is preaching his very first sermon, he looks at the people around him in Jerusalem and says, "This Jesus, delivered up according to the definite plan and foreknowledge of God, you crucified and killed by the hands of lawless men" (Acts 2:23). On the one hand, it was absolutely certain that Jesus Christ was going to die, and at the same time, those who crucified him are utterly responsible for what they did. What you do matters, and you are responsible for it.

What this really means, on the one hand, is that God is completely in charge, no matter how bad things get, and, on the other hand, what you do matters. I know that intellectually we say:

"How can they both be right? It seems that if God is in charge, it doesn't matter what I do. If it really matters what I do, then what's going to happen can't really be set in God's plan." I know how difficult that is to reconcile logically, but I want you to realize how incredibly practical it is at the lived-life level to believe what the Bible says.

Take prayer, for example. If you really believe that your prayers can change the plan of God, and if you ever pray again, then you're not thinking things through. You have far too high a view of your own wisdom. Here is what I have said numerous times before, especially to younger people: when you're ten years old, you think your eight-year-old self was totally stupid. When you're fifteen years old, you think back to your ten-year-old self and the things you wrote and believed, and you go, "Ugh." When you're twenty years old, you think your fifteen-year-old self was a jerk. When you're thirty, you really think your twenty-year-old self was a jerk. Guess what? You're a jerk right now. You just haven't realized it yet.

Therefore, on the one hand, if you really believed that your prayers could change the will of God—change the plan of God— you should never pray again. How do you know what should happen? You don't. On the other hand, if you just believe everything is fated and it doesn't matter how we live, then you have no incentive to stretch every nerve. But the Bible says that what you do matters. You are responsible. And at the same time, you can't completely screw up your life because God is in charge. You need to know that. You need to know that both are true, or you won't be able to live life. That's why the people who crucified Jesus Christ were guilty, and, at the same time, it was absolutely certain he was going to die for our sins.

A City under Attack

Here's a second thing we learn from Nehemiah 4: it almost seems to be a principle that when you're doing something good for God, you will be attacked somehow. Jesus Christ is baptized; the Spirit comes down; God says, "This is my beloved Son, with whom I am well pleased" (Matt. 3:16–17)—that's clearly a high point. The next thing you know, he's in the wilderness being tempted by the Devil (4:1–11). Likewise, Elijah experiences a great triumph over the prophets of Baal, fire comes down from heaven on Mount Carmel, he outruns a chariot—and then he gets incredibly depressed (1 Kings 18:20–19:4).

That is the Christian life. You see it over and over again. Why? If you identify with Jesus Christ, you're going to be persecuted. Here is the beatitude we all hate: "Blessed are you when people insult you, persecute you and falsely say all kinds of evil against you because of me. Rejoice and be glad, because great is your reward in heaven, for in the same way they persecuted the prophets who were before you" (Matt. 5:11–12 NIV). And, of course, 2 Timothy 3:12: "All who desire to live a godly life in Christ Jesus will be persecuted." All. You are going to get this kind of mockery and disdain. "Hear us, our God, for we are despised" (Neh. 4:4a). One thing that has not changed a bit is that we are despised, and we are despised for the sake of the Lord.

Now, there are two things to be said before we go to the medicine chest for this—the place of remedies. First, it's interesting to notice that the founders of the other great religions did not die in shame. Buddha, Mohammed, Confucius—they had a lot of problems, but from what we know, they died old, full of years, and surrounded by admirers. In many ways, they triumphed. Jesus Christ died young, cut off, and in shame. Why? I think it was because, at the human level, his claims were so much greater.

Anne Rice, who wrote The Vampire Chronicles, was writing a novel about Christianity some years ago. Like most novelists, she was trying to study her subject, and she started reading New Testament scholarship. She was astounded by the fact that so many of the people in the world of history and New Testament scholarship actually seemed to dislike the person they were studying. This is what she said:

Many of these scholars, scholars who apparently devoted their life to New Testament scholarship, disliked Jesus Christ. Some pitied him as a hopeless failure. Others sneered at him, and some felt an outright contempt. . . . I'd never come across this kind of emotion in any other field of research, at least not to this extent. It was puzzling. The people who go into Elizabethan studies don't set out to prove that Queen Elizabeth I was a fool. They don't personally dislike her. They don't make snickering remarks about her, or spend their careers trying to pick apart her historical reputation. . . . Occasionally a scholar studies a villain, yes. But even then, the author generally ends up arguing for the good points of a villain or for his or her place in history. . . . But in general scholars don't spend their lives in the company of historical figures whom they openly despise. But there are New Testament scholars who detest and despise Jesus Christ.[3]

The point is that if you identify with Jesus Christ, you will be despised. Those of us in Western societies are certainly in for a lot more despising than we have had in a long time.

Second, what should we do when that happens? Here's the answer. Don't say: "Hear us, our God, for we are despised. . . . Do *not* cover up their guilt or blot out their sins from your sight, for they have thrown insults in the face of the builders" (Neh. 4:4–5).

Derek Kidner, who wrote a commentary on Ezra and Nehemiah, also wrote a wonderful commentary on Psalms, in which he talks about the imprecatory psalms—the ones that say such things as, "Lord, blot them out. . . . Don't forgive them. . . . Don't cover their guilt."[4] For example, in Psalm 137, the psalmist says to the Babylonians: "Blessed shall he be who repays you with what you have done to us! Blessed shall he be who takes your little ones and

---

[3] Anne Rice, *Christ the Lord: Out of Egypt* (New York: Random House, Ballantine Books, 2006), author's note, 332–33.
[4] Derek Kidner, *Psalms 1–72: An Introduction and Commentary*, Vol. 1, Tyndale Old Testament Commentaries (1973; repr., London: Inter-Varsity, 2008), 39–47. The second volume covers the rest of the psalms.

dashes them against the rock!" (vv. 8–9). That's what the Babylonians did in those days when sacking a city. They would find the infants in the city they were invading, grab them by the feet, and dash their brains out on a rock. So the psalmist says, "Oh, Lord, let that happen to them."

Kidner says we need to remember three things when we read psalms such as this. First, these are cries against injustice. Christians today should still cry out against injustice. We should tell God about it and ask him to do something. He's a God of justice. We shouldn't just give in and say, "That's life." Second, even in the Old Testament, those who are praying are almost always not taking vengeance themselves. They are saying, "Lord, you take it." But, third, Kidner says that on this side of the cross, Christians don't pray like that, and I think he's right.

Why? Because we know this: God's little one had his head dashed. He was stricken. He was crucified and despised so that we could have a name that will never die. Our reputations, our names, are secure. We can't really be despised, not in the long run, because our names are written in heaven. Why? Because he was despised. He made himself of no reputation. He emptied himself of all his glory. He got all kinds of persecution, so now, when it happens to us—when we are despised—we can say, "Lord, I look to you for my vindication," which is actually what Nehemiah did. But we have resources to forgive our enemies—to love our enemies—that Nehemiah did not have.

There's a sense in which Jesus is saying something like this: "Look, if you take a little hit to your reputation, if you get persecuted a little bit, knowing what I did for you, you can take it. I got the ultimate shame. I was rejected, even by my Father. I got the shame and rejection you deserved so that now you know your name is written in heaven. You're a citizen of the ultimate city. You're surrounded by the ultimate walls of salvation. You can't lose that because you're mine. You can handle it. You're part of God's people—all ministers and all one. Speak up for me. Pray and post a guard. Do my work, and if you are despised, know that those who look to me will never be put to shame."

Reflect and Pray

Reflect on each question, and then take a moment to speak or write the prayers that grow from those reflections.

1. Nehemiah 3 paints a beautiful picture of God's people fully engaged, working side by side to rebuild the Jerusalem wall. The task required all the people, with their various skills. Similarly, every Christian has a ministry and particular gifts needed for the building up of the church. What ministry has the Lord given you during this season of your life, and how are you using the gifts he has given you? Give thanks for a couple of people whom you're glad to have beside you.

2. The rebuilding work met with serious opposition, as Nehemiah 4 vividly portrays. What stands out to you about the way God's people responded to this opposition? What are some unhelpful ways they might have been tempted to respond, but didn't?

3. Tim Keller reminds us that we too face serious opposition as those who identify with Jesus Christ. The New Testament everywhere affirms the cost of following Jesus in a hostile world. Read 1 Peter 4:12–19. How does this passage encourage you toward perseverance and joy in the work of ministry?

Think Like an Expositor

Consider how many different ways Tim Keller sets the gospel before us in this chapter. He's clearly about not just expounding Nehemiah, but also about showing how to expound Nehemiah in light of the gospel. In his book *Preaching: Communicating Faith in an Age of Skepticism*, he commends the guiding principle of keeping the gospel at the center of a message, for the sake of nonbelievers as well as believers:

The key . . . to addressing at the same time both those who believe and those who do not—and even subgroups within cultures—is to go down to the heart level and call for gospel motivation in your preaching. It *is* impossible to address Christians and non-Christians at once if you misunderstand the gospel's versatility and centrality to life. The gospel is not just the means by which people get converted but also the way Christians solve their problems and grow. The typical approach to the gospel is to see it as the "ABC's" of Christian doctrine only, the minimum truth required to be saved, the admissions test, the entry point. Then it is understood that we make progress in the Christian life through the application of other (more advanced) biblical principles. If that were the case, then of course we could not do both evangelism and spiritual formation at the same time. Yet the gospel not only is the way we are saved but also is always the solution to every problem and the way to advance at every stage in the Christian life.[5]

This, of course, means that to preach or teach any text faithfully, one must preach or teach Christ: "You can't properly preach any text—putting it into its rightful place in the whole Bible—unless you show how its themes find their fulfillment in the person of Christ. Likewise, you can't really reach and restructure the affections of the heart unless you point through the biblical principles to the beauty of Jesus himself, showing clearly how the particular truth in your text can be practiced only through faith in the work of Christ."[6]

Keller is well known for being able to reach out with the gospel to the surrounding culture. This chapter is a good example of why. It's not just that he thinks expansively and draws in illustrations that speak to our experiences, doubts, and struggles today—although that is without doubt true. It certainly does wake us up and draw us in, for example, to hear him quoting Anne Rice, the

---

[5] Timothy Keller, *Preaching: Communicating Faith in an Age of Skepticism* (New York: Viking, 2015), 118–19.
[6] Ibid, 22.

author of The Vampire Chronicles, concerning those who despise the person of Christ.

But the reaching out connects with listeners finally because it is only the truth and the person of Christ himself that enliven and transform the heart. This is a good confidence for any teacher to hold strong and clear: that, as we lift up Christ—as *the Word of God* from start to finish lifts up Christ—he will do his sovereign work in people's hearts, by his Spirit and his Word. "Preaching Christ is not only the ultimate way to fully understand a text, nor just the best way to simultaneously reach those who don't believe and those who do, but also the way to be sure that your address moves beyond a dry lecture and becomes a real proclamation of the truth that reaches the heart."[7]

---

[7] Ibid., 178–79.

3

Fearing God in a Fallen World

Nehemiah 5-6

Paige Brown

Though I'm sure that John Newton wrote the second stanza of his most famous hymn to express the convicting and converting power of grace in his own life, he unwittingly did us a secondary favor. His language suggests for us the great lessons to be learned from Nehemiah 5 and 6. Newton wrote:

> 'Twas grace that taught my heart to fear,
> and grace my fears relieved;
> how precious did that grace appear
> the hour I first believed![1]

'Twas Grace That Taught My Heart to Fear

What do we see in Nehemiah specifically about the *fear* that grace teaches?

---

[1] From "Amazing Grace" by John Newton, 1776.

Foundational

In the first place, it is foundational. The fear of God, which is a huge concept in the Scriptures, is the awe, the reverence, the honor, and the worship demanded by the majesty of his person, his power, and his position. This fear is the only proper response to the God of the Bible. He is, of course, to be before all things in our hearts, because he is before all things in reality. Therefore, this fear is supremely rational.

So it makes sense when Proverbs tells us repeatedly that the fear of the Lord is the beginning of wisdom (1:7; 9:10). If you have done broad-stroke study of the Old Testament, then you know that the fear of God, or the fear of the Lord, is the theme and controlling principle of all the Wisdom Literature—which figures, because there could be no wisdom without it. We talk about the fear of God in the modern parlance of "getting it." For example, "She's really smart, but she just doesn't get it." The Wisdom Literature is always asking, "Do you *get* it?" We can know many things and be quite intelligent, but if our knowledge is not founded upon and encased in the fear of God, then we just don't get it.

I got up one Saturday morning when I was in the tenth grade. I sharpened my No. 2 pencils and walked down to the high school for the PSAT—the Preliminary Scholastic Aptitude Test, which determines National Merit Scholarships. Taking the first section, as the administrator repeatedly called out the time, I was right on schedule. When we had one minute left, I was answering the last question of that section, number 70. But as I looked down, ready to fill in my circle for that question, I saw that it was already filled in on my Scantron sheet. I started going back over the filled-in circles in a panic. Where had I skipped? As the administrator called, "Time!" I found out that I had skipped the answer line of the third question. So I grabbed my sharp pencils and walked home without even bothering to take the other two parts of the test. I am a National *De*-Merit finalist. And though I have no corroborating witnesses, I'm sure that I had all the answers right. We can be really smart. We can know lots of stuff. We can know all the right answers. But they will all be in the wrong place if the fear of God is not in the *first* place. It is foundational.

And it is foundational for Nehemiah. His prayer in chapter 1 is the catalyst for the entire book. In it, Nehemiah in effect says to the Lord: "I come to you primarily as one who fears your name. That's who I am." He confesses his sin and the sin of his people before this holy God from whom they have turned and whose judgment they have experienced through years of exile (vv. 6–7). He claims God's covenant love for a sinful people (vv. 8–10). And he echoes his fear of God with the great doctrinal names for God he scatters throughout the book: "the great and awesome God" (1:5; cf. 4:14; 9:32) and "the God of heaven" (2:20). His words reflect understanding of a majestic God, the one self-sustaining eternal God, worshiped by the multitudes of heaven. As we would say, "Nehemiah *gets* it."

Wisdom is required in . . . *everything*. What topics do Proverbs and Ecclesiastes cover? Almost every one you can think of, because wisdom is required in everything. Therefore, the fear of God is *foundational* to everything. It is a perpetual posture. It is not an occasional exercise.

My sister is prissy. We actually come from the same biological parents. And she is prissy. She was born prissy. I don't mean that she only dresses up prissy or that she socializes prissy. She exercises prissy. She works in the yard prissy. She unloads groceries prissy. She doesn't merely act a certain way. She *is* a certain way. Nehemiah does not perform tasks in the fear of the Lord; he *lives* in the fear of the Lord. It is his perpetual posture, but not as drudgery, not even as a duty. He declares in 1:11 that he and others are "your servants who delight to fear your name," echoing the words of the sage, "Blessed is the one who fears the LORD always" (Prov. 28:14). 'Twas grace that taught his heart to fear. And that fear is foundational.

Relational

Second, the fear that grace teaches is relational. It's strange to think of fear as relational instead of anti-relational. After all, wasn't fear the original effect of sin? The first thing that post-fall Adam says to God is, "I heard you coming and I was *afraid*, so I hid" (see Gen. 3:10). That broken relationship immediately led to fear—fear of God's judgment. Newton clearly understood this fear that exposes our sin and our need of rescue from God's wrath; such fear needs *relief*.

Such fear comes by God's grace, to awaken us to him, and such fear is relieved by God's grace, to restore us to right relationship with him. The gracious restoration of a right relationship through God's covenant with his people is the story of the rest of the Bible. This restoration is signified powerfully for us in the possessive personal pronouns that fill the story. As Martin Luther famously said, "The heart of Christianity lies in its personal pronouns." God says: "I will be *your* God. You will be *my* people." In Nehemiah 5 and 6, we see these telling personal pronouns actually applied to fear. So, is fear a result of the broken relationship? Or is fear a result of the restored relationship?

Obviously there are distinctions that need to be made, and Luther again helpfully explains them to us. Luther distinguished between a *servile* fear, which is the dread and terror that a prisoner in a torture chamber feels for his tormentor or executioner, and a *filial* fear, which is family fear. It is the love and adoration of a child for a father whom he so dearly wants to please. He feels fear not because he has any dread or terror of punishment, but because he is eager to avoid displeasing or offending that one who is the source of his security and love.[2] A servile fear is appropriate for those not belonging to God; a filial fear replaces that servile fear and then characterizes those who are the people of God.

We see this distinction made clearly for us biblically in Exodus

---

[2] Martin Luther, quoted in "Fostering Fear of God," in Devotionals, http://www.ligonier.org/learn/devotionals/fostering-fear-god/

20. The Israelites are filled with fear as God is visibly present on Mount Sinai. Moses says to them, "Do not fear, for God has come to test you, that the fear of him may be before you, that you may not sin" (v. 20). In other words, "Have no servile fear, for God has come to us to give us, his children, the privilege of family fear." Nehemiah also makes this distinction in his use of covenant language. He applies personal pronouns to fear and talks about the fear of "*our* God," the fear of "*my* God." According to Nehemiah, these people are "*your* servants who delight to fear *your* name" (1:11).

So Nehemiah's fear is not only foundational, showing that he has a proper recognition of God, but also relational, showing that he *belongs* to God. As Isaiah says, "The fear of the LORD is Zion's treasure" (Isa. 33:6). And we find in Nehemiah that this treasured fear is not only inflaming his love for the Lord, but also his love for the Lord's people. The personal pronouns and filial language extend to them. In chapter 5, all of his anger and confronting, all of his urging and pleading, are because the victims are "*our brothers.*" He is asking, "How can we do this to our brothers?" All the family language, all the possessive language, applies to these oppressed people.

The fear of God extends blessing to his family, our family, and in this story, the family is at risk. Therefore, everything stops until this problem is dealt with. Nehemiah cannot sacrifice the people to the walls. The walls are for the people. So he does not privately take them to court. He calls the entire assembly together so that they can see each other face to face, to charge that the accused are acting like pawnbrokers and not like brothers.[3] His concern is for the oppressed and for the oppressors, because they are brothers. He calls together the assembly, then measures them and himself not only against the legalities, but also against that relationship. The fear of our God must determine the treatment of our brothers and sisters.

---

[3] Derek Kidner, *Ezra and Nehemiah: An Introduction & Commentary*, Tyndale Old Testament Commentaries (Downers Grove, IL: InterVarsity Press, 1979), 96.

God is using Nehemiah to build his walls, yes—but more importantly, to build his people, because they are his permanent possession. Jerusalem is a birth canal; it's an incubator. It will pass away. The people are the permanent possession. Nehemiah understands that because of his relational fear. Nehemiah is not just doing a job. He's serving the Lord by tangibly serving his people.

I was on a field trip to a museum in downtown Dallas with students from an inner-city school with which I was involved in my years there. The headmaster had left a successful law career to come and take the helm at this school. As we were coming back through the city, he called out to the bus driver to pull over in front of a courthouse. The middle school girl sitting next to me said, "Why are we stopping?"

The headmaster replied, "I want you to see this courthouse because I've spent so much time here."

Her eyes grew big: "You got *arrested?*"

"No . . ."

"You're a *cop?*"

"No, I'm a lawyer."

"You got *fired?*"

And he said, "No, I quit."

She raised her eyebrows, "Why?"

Without pause he replied, "So I could be with *you.*"

I wish I had a picture of the thrilled and teased look on her face in that moment.

Nehemiah can look at these people and say, "I left it all so I could be with you, so I could serve you, because the fear of my God has let me know how important you are." 'Twas grace that taught his heart to fear. The fear that filled Nehemiah was foundational and relational.

Motivational

Third, the fear that grace teaches is motivational. We find theologian John Murray's well-known chapter on the "Fear of God" not in his *Principles of the Devotional Mind.* We find it in his classic work *Principles of Conduct,* because he makes it very clear that the fear of God is not only the soul of godliness, it is also the motivation for *conduct,* for active obedience.[4]

In C. S. Lewis's *The Screwtape Letters,* Uncle Screwtape gives his nephew Wormwood excellent advice about keeping his human "patient"—as he is called in the book—from making any spiritual progress. Screwtape writes:

> Keep his mind on the inner life. He thinks his conversion is something inside him. . . . The great thing is to prevent his doing anything. As long as he does not convert it into action, it does not matter how much he thinks. . . . Let him do anything but act. No amount of piety in his imaginations and affections will harm us if we can keep them out of his will. The more often he feels without acting, the less he will ever be able to act.[5]

Nehemiah would be an outrageously frustrating "patient" to such demons, because the fear of the Lord comes spilling out of his mind and heart as the irrepressible motivation for drastic actions of justice and mercy. The text tells us he gets "very angry" (5:6). He is emotionally involved here. But he doesn't just get very angry. He acts. The poor are suffering under hard times, as well as hard hearts. He calls together the entire assembly and deals with the problem.

There is no situational ethic here; fearing God affects everything. From "Let's get internationally strong and secure" to "Let's jeopardize all of that to take care of our own poor," Nehemiah's priorities are God's priorities. What good would it be to build external walls around internal corruption? It's got to stop. The job cannot trump that which is near and dear to the Lord. So he calls the people—everyone—to a higher standard. And with what

---

[4] John Murray, *Principles of Conduct: Aspects of Biblical Ethics* (Grand Rapids, MI: Eerdmans, 1957).

[5] C. S. Lewis, *The Screwtape Letters* (New York: MacMillan, 1961), 16, 60.

motivation? "Ought you not to walk in the fear of our God?" (v. 9). In other words, "Is the fear of our God not motivating us to more than this?" That motivation, he is saying, should take them beyond the law-keeping of no slavery and no usury, all the way to generosity. "Let's give it all back!" And no, there's no indication that Nehemiah is actually breaking the law. It appears that he is just lending capital. Derek Kidner points out that he's including himself, not criminally, but heartlessly, saying that the nobles and officials should be making gifts, not loans.[6] No one should ever benefit from the needs and the sufferings of brothers. We should bear their needs with them.

In case they don't take him seriously enough, Nehemiah truly "puts the fear of God in them" as he calls in the priests and makes them swear to do as they have promised, and then gives them a visible curse of "shaking out" his garment just for emphasis (v. 13). "You had better take this seriously," he is saying. "We are talking about the fear of our God and what that demands."

Nehemiah then makes a parenthesis in this chapter to talk about his own long-term move beyond generosity, all the way to sacrifice (vv. 14–19). For twelve years as their governor, he has not taken the food allowance or his stipend because it would be burdensome for the people. And he doesn't just shut his doors and live lean, but rather fills his table up with 150 people every day, paid for at his own expense. Why? Because taking care of him would be too heavy for them, so he takes care of them (v. 18). Why does he do that? Verse 15: because of the fear of God.

Likewise motivated to unwavering perseverance, Nehemiah is committed rightly to getting the job done. Within ten months (that's not very long) of his hearing in the Citadel of Susa about the plight of Jerusalem, the wall is finished. Fifty-two days of work and it is *done*.

We like to talk about Nehemiah as that rare man of action,

---

[6] Kidner, *Ezra and Nehemiah*, 96.

envisioning a cape, broad shoulders, and a skinny waist. We like to talk about his extraordinary calling and his extraordinary ability. But Nehemiah himself tells us that all he did was because of the fear of God. His was an extraordinary time, yes. His was an extraordinary situation in which to live out our *ordinary* motivation. We want to say "I'm a thinker, I'm a reader, I'm a studier, I'm an advisor, I'm just not a doer." But a godly fearer is a doer. The fear of God always motivates our living and our doing. The fear of God is not a contemplation. It is a motivation.

Corrie ten Boom's book *The Hiding Place* has been the most important book of my life since I was young. I think that's because it's the story of that completely ordinary Dutch family made so unbelievably extraordinary by their commitment to the Lord and what he placed in front of them. Before they were arrested, before they built the secret room in their home, the Nazis invaded Holland, banning Jewish citizens there from freely walking the streets. So Corrie began picking up and delivering her family's watch shop work for Jewish customers in their homes. One evening, she was on such an errand in the home of a doctor and his family:

> They were a very old Dutch family, the portraits on the walls could have been a textbook of Holland's history. The Heemstras and I were talking about the things that were discussed whenever a group of people got together in those days, when down the stairs piped a childish voice, "Daddy! You didn't tuck us in!"
>
> Dr. Heemstra was on his feet in an instant. With an apology to his wife and me, he hurried upstairs and in a minute we heard a game of hide-and-seek going and the shrill laughter of two children. That was all. Nothing had changed. Mrs. Heemstra continued with her recipe for stretching the tea ration with rose leaves. And yet everything was changed. For in that instant, reality broke through the numbness that had grown in me since the invasion. At any minute, there might be a rap

on this door. These children, this mother and father, might be ordered to the back of a truck.

Dr. Heemstra came back to the living room and the conversation rambled on, but under the words a prayer was forming in my heart, "Lord Jesus, I offer myself for your people in any way, any place, any time."[7]

Think of the lives that our God saved through that prayer and the lives that he has blessed through that prayer, including my own. Has the fear of the Lord motivated a prayer like that in our hearts? "Lord Jesus, I offer myself for your work in any way, any place, any time." That seems to be the ongoing prayer of Nehemiah's heart because he mentions *walking* in the fear of the Lord (5:9). Walking involves the way that we move all the time and everywhere. It's normative for us. The fear of the Lord is to be normative for us, and yet it inevitably brings the abnormal into the normal.

It is not the fear of God unless we, at various times, are motivated to do what we would never do otherwise. I get it into my mind that the people who are really about God's business just naturally love it, right? But did Noah like animals? Did Moses like camping? Did Ruth like gleaning? Did Daniel like living abroad? Did John the Baptist like confrontation? Did Paul like prison? Did Nehemiah like construction? These people did not love their assignments. They feared the Lord. And those were the assignments *he* gave them. That's the motivation—not the love for the thing, but *the fear of the Lord*. 'Twas grace that taught all those hearts to fear. That fear was foundational, relational, and motivational.

Resignational

Fourth, the fear that grace teaches is resignational (sometimes you just have to make up words). Chapters 5 and 6, like others throughout the book of Nehemiah, are punctuated with Nehe-

---

[7] Corrie ten Boom, *The Hiding Place* (Westwood, NJ: Barbour, 1971), 73.

miah's very brief prayers—"arrow prayers," as they have been called. These are perhaps most revealing about Nehemiah's fear of the Lord, as in them he is constantly looking to the Lord for strength and safety, for reward and revenge. He *resigns* himself solely and wholly unto God.

Look at the prayer in 5:19, which might sound a little strange to us: "Remember for my good, O my God, all that I have done for this people." We don't know if the people are even fully aware of all Nehemiah has done. That's not what Nehemiah cares about. Nehemiah is not publicly doing the ESPN endzone dance for the highlight replays. There is no plaque noting his philanthropy. There is no advertisement of his sponsorship. There are no place cards at the table saying, "Generously donated by . . ." He is seeking reward only in the approval of God.

Perhaps you have heard what I heard as I swooped down to lift my six-year-old daughter in a tight embrace after her dance recital. I said, "Baby, everybody thought you were great!" She leaned back, gave me a seriously piercing look, and immediately asked, "But what did *you* think?" Nehemiah cares only what the Lord thinks because he has done it all for only one reason: to please God. And we know that it did, because the psalmist promises, "The LORD takes pleasure in those who fear him" (Ps. 147:11). Matthew Henry says: "If men forget me, let my God think on me and I desire no more. His thoughts us-ward are our happiness."[8]

Look at the prayer in 6:14: "Remember Tobiah and Sanballat, O my God, according to these things that they did, and also . . . the rest of the prophets who wanted to make me afraid." He prays against his enemies, but he doesn't prescribe against his enemies. He leaves that to the Lord. "Lord, this is your work, and these are your enemies to deal with. I have no punishments to suggest for them any more than I have rewards to suggest for myself. I

---

[8] Matthew Henry, *Commentary on the Whole Bible*, Vol. 2 (Peabody, MA: Hendrickson, 1991), 838.

am looking to you as the avenger. I am looking only to you as the judge."

Look at the prayer in 6:9: "O God, strengthen my hands." Consider the catalog of personal attacks in these chapters. There is intimidation. There is sabotage. There are threats. There is slander. And yet, Nehemiah's prayer is not, "Lord, change this!" What is it? "Lord, strengthen *me.* Silence my fears and make me strong in you." Perhaps even in that arrow prayer he had in mind these words from Isaiah:

> Strengthen the weak hands,
>   and make firm the feeble knees.
> Say to those who have an anxious heart,
>   "Be strong; fear not!
> Behold, your God
>   will come with vengeance,
> with the recompense of God.
> He will come and save you." (Isa. 35:3–4)

Nehemiah is running only to the Lord for strength, success, and safety. These prayers are a sampling of resignational fear. Nehemiah's confidence is nowhere but in God. We do not know what will happen. He didn't either. But we know who God is. We know the redemption he has promised. We know that he has us, that we belong to him, that it all belongs to him. Nehemiah knew that too.

Our friends Doug and Masha Shepherd have been living and working for many years in Ukraine. As you can imagine, that has been a very interesting and stressful place to work in the midst of the ongoing tensions between Ukraine and Russia. Their recent newsletter recounted the scene of their two-year-old dressing herself for a trip to the market with Masha. She put on summer stretch pants and a winter coat, a hat and rain boots, and her mom's sunglasses. Doug wrote:

> Sophia unknowingly represented exactly what daily life has become in Ukraine for many. Since we don't know what to

expect in the country, we mentally prepare for all options. This mental calibration of expectations across a wide spectrum is *exhausting*. The daily routine of rainboots and sunglasses forces a few basic questions: Will the day bring sunshine or rain? Which means will there be bloodshed or peace? Will the country disintegrate or rise up to defend herself? With every dawn we prepare to put on our expectations for all scenarios. This daily exercise is truly a blessing for the believer even in the uncertainty of a day filled with the horrors of the fallen world. . . . We have been moving from the fear of the "what ifs" to the faith in "Who is." So, in the end we still face the unknown of every day, but now we more easily slide the sunglasses and rainboots on in faith and deep trust that our Father is good.[9]

Sunglasses and rainboots. We don't know that the Lord will change that. Lord, strengthen me. There are no "what ifs" in his world. He is our hiding place and our safety. Can we resign our hearts with Nehemiah and rest there? 'Twas grace that taught his heart that fear—that foundational, relational, motivational, and resignational fear.

. . . And Grace My Fears Relieved

The order of Newton's lyrics has to be the order in Nehemiah's life. Fear is like coveting. We are never commanded not to covet. We are commanded not to covet earthly things, which can be prevented only by coveting the things of the Lord. In the same way, we are never commanded not to fear. We are commanded not to fear earthly things, which can be prevented only by *fearing the Lord*. Notice Paul's order in Colossians 3: first set your mind and heart on things above; only then can you put to death what is earthly in you (vv. 1–5). Likewise, set your *fear* on God above. Only then can you deal with what is below *without fear*.

---

[9] Doug Shepherd, "Lviv Newsletter," April 2014.

To paraphrase Thomas Chalmers, this is the expulsive power of a new fear, a better fear.

The question is: What is expelled? Or, to use Newton's word, what is "relieved"? 'Twas grace that taught my heart to fear. Then grace my *fears* relieved. Fears—that's plural. There are too many fears to cover here. The first great fear is of the judgment of God's wrath. But then, once that fear is relieved by God's saving grace, other fears still threaten, even for those who live in relationship with him. What fears do we see specifically in our chapters, fears that are relieved for Nehemiah by the ongoing grace of God in his life?

Self-Promoting Fears

In the first place are the self-promoting fears. Nehemiah refuses to be driven by the fears that always accompany getting ahead—financially, vocationally, politically. And he has had golden opportunities to get ahead.

Financially, he could have made a killing with his resources to lend and to invest, and with his position to enforce and to capitalize upon. But he has no "business is business" attitude. Instead, he is giving instead of lending. He is sacrificing instead of collecting, even his own salary. The instantaneous way for you and me to know where our hearts are is to look right now at where our money is. So says the Lord Jesus himself: where your treasure is determines where your heart is (Luke 12:34). And when we look to see where that is, and what took our hearts there, what do we find? Is it grasping? Is it panic? Is it greed? Is it all selfish spending? What is driving our finances? Is it self-promoting fears? The grace-taught fear of the Lord relieves them.

What about vocationally? Nehemiah was willing to jeopardize his whole flagship enterprise, go head to head with his greatest contributors and leaders, and enforce their generosity to the clerical workers and cleaning staff members. That is hardly the way to get ahead. What is driving our jobs—paid and unpaid? What is driving our ambitions? What is driving our work? Is it our self-promoting fears? Is that why we perform for whom we do? Is that why we ignore and belittle whom we do? Is that why we pursue certain people? Is that why we resent anyone who competes with us or gets in our way, even in ministry (or especially in ministry)? Are those things driven by our self-promoting fears?

The job of leading the rebuilding of Jerusalem is a huge deal to Nehemiah. He sacrificed his plum position, left his home, and came halfway across the known world, and is risking his life. The job is huge to him. But it's not as big as God he is now to him. It's not that our jobs are to be unimportant. They are to be *less* important. For Nehemiah, the grace-taught fear of the Lord relieved all of those fears that we would expect in somebody so committed to his work.

What about politically and socially? Nehemiah has been given ripe chances to get ahead with the neighboring provinces. He has been given ripe chances to get ahead with his own nobles and officials. He has been given ripe chances to get ahead with Tobiah. He has been given ripe chances to get ahead with the king. And he is constantly doing what will put him behind. He is indicting his ablest men in their treatment of the poor and demanding that they do something about it. He is ignoring and offending the powerful neighboring provinces that oppose the Lord. He is ignoring Tobiah and those powerfully allied with him in his own midst. Nehemiah is willing to make internal and external enemies to follow the Lord.

Self-promotion means using people rather than loving them. And then we have to be very selective, if not fickle, about who is useful to us. Fearing the Lord means we do not get to choose whom to please and whom to offend. That is not left up to us. Nehemiah is not catering to anyone; he is not climbing any ladder; he is willing to be lonely and misunderstood. What is driving our social life? What is driving our relationships? What is driving our commitments? Is it self-promoting fears? Is that why we socialize with whom we do and politely blow off whom we do? Is that why we dress a certain way? Is that why we laugh at certain things? Is that why we have the memberships that we do? Is that why we care so terribly much about how our kids fit in and look and perform? The grace-taught fear of the Lord relieves these fears. It relieves the self-promotion and all of the fears that drive it.

Perhaps the most insidious form of this fear is manifested when we use the very things of the Lord to promote *self*. That would have been so easy for Nehemiah.

I have friends who moved from a desirable part of the suburbs into an impoverished part of their city with their four children. Three of the kids were on board and felt great about it, but the six-year-old was a bit more resentful, if not resistant. But several months into the adventure, she walked into the kitchen to announce, "Mommy, I wanna give all my birthday money to the poor people." Her mother almost dropped the dish she was drying. She thought she could hear the angels singing. But before she could even respond, "Baby, that's so great!" she heard, "Now, Mommy, if I do this, can I go on that Oprah show and tell everybody about it?"

It would be so understandable if Nehemiah were saying, "If I'm going to obey on all these fronts, can't I at least let everybody know about it so they see that I'm a rock star?" It is so hard for us not to advertise. And yet the need to advertise, *even* our relationship with the Lord, comes from the self-promoting fears infiltrating our relationship with the Lord. That's why he says you don't advertise your prayer life—rather, you go into your closet in secret. You don't advertise your giving—even with yourself, so that your right hand doesn't know what your left hand is doing. He doesn't say *if* you fast; he assumes that we will. So *when* you fast, you do not advertise it even with a facial expression to indicate what you are doing (see Matt. 6:1–18). In Colossians 3:22, Paul encourages obedience "not by way of eye-service, as people pleasers, but with sincerity of heart, *fearing the Lord*." We are reading Nehemiah's personal journal, not flyers on public bulletin boards. He did not go on the Oprah show. Self-promoting fears will always be driven by what will make me look best, sound best, and seem best in the situation. This explains our inconsistencies—because what will make me look best, sound best, and seem best in any situation changes even hourly, so that we change accordingly.

The question for all of us is: Are we known as God-fearers, in whatever context, conversation, relationship, or situation? Nehemiah is fully consistent as he leans upon the Lord and looks only to him in fear. The Lord has said, "Fear not, I am with you . . . I will uphold you with my righteous right hand" (Isa. 41:10). He doesn't say, "I will pull you through." He says, "I will *uphold* you." There's no need for self-promotion. God is doing that for us. So Nehemiah's self-promoting fears are relieved.

Self-Protecting Fears

But what about self-protecting fears? Not trying to get ahead, just trying to be safe—just trying to survive. Some of the attacks on Nehemiah are actually life-threatening. All of them are personally discouraging and aimed at personal destruction: the demand for a summit again and again; the *open-letter* accusation of rebellion and treason; the treacherous alliances of the nobility with Tobiah; the public voices of the false prophets speaking against him; his friends, his people, his clergy turning against him. Nehemiah doesn't even know how to tell enemy from friend. And he comments repeatedly that it was "to make me afraid. . . . It was to frighten me. . . . It was to frighten us." His situation has to be exhausting.

The kids and I went over to a dear friend's house for a play-date late one afternoon, and as we walked in, her three-year-old came walking through. He had the Cheetos stain all around his mouth, his pacifier in, his blanky over his shoulder, Diet Coke in his sippy cup in one hand, and the remote control in the other hand. I couldn't help but laugh as his mother said: "I know, I know. I promise you I am so firm with him until nine o'clock every morning. After that, he just *wears me down!*" We can all relate.

The situation in Jerusalem has to be wearing Nehemiah down. They ask him, they pressure him, they ask him, they pressure him. And yet, he does not waver. It is one thing to have a conviction, and it's another thing to stand by it. Nehemiah's resolve is not battling his fears; his *fear* is battling his fears. Look again at both aspects of Nehemiah's reaction in chapter 6. In response to a warning, "They are coming to kill you. They are coming to kill you by night" (v. 10), he fires back: "Should such a man as I run away?" (v. 11). And in response to, "Let us meet together in the house of God, within the temple. Let us close the doors of the temple, for they are coming to kill you" (v. 10), he quickly says, "What man such as I could go into the temple and live?" (v. 11). "I know whom to be afraid of," Nehemiah is saying. "I am not afraid of them, yet I am far too fearful of God to go in there and commit that grave desecration against the Lord." Nehemiah lives just as Jesus said: "Do not fear those who kill the body but cannot kill the soul. Rather fear him who can destroy both soul and body in hell" (Matt. 10:28).

Nehemiah's greatest fear is not death; it is offending the Lord. He sounds just like Shadrach, Meshach, and Abednego giving it to King Nebuchadnezzar: "Our God whom we serve is able to deliver us from the burning fiery furnace, and he will deliver us out of your hand, O king. But if not, be it known to you, O king, that we will not serve your gods or worship the golden image that you have set up" (Dan. 3:17–18). Nehemiah fears sinning more than he fears dying. But his fear is not overcoming his reason. His is the only *rational* fear—it has the ultimate *reason*. The command "Do not fear" in Scripture (it is there more than three hundred times) always follows or is followed by the reason: "Because I am the Lord. . . . Because I will fight for you. . . . Because I am with you. . . . Because I have promised you. . . . Because I hold you." In other words, "The reason you should not fear is not ever because of you, but because of *me*." Instead of being overcome by fears, Nehemiah overcomes by fear.

The church father known to us as John Chrysostom was the bishop of Constantinople around AD 400. He earned the name Chrysostom, meaning "the golden mouth," because of his preaching ability. The story is often told that the emperor, worn out with Chrysostom's golden mouth and tired of his pointed preaching, called him in to threaten him with exile unless he changed his message. Chrysostom reportedly replied, "You cannot banish me, for this world is my Father's house."

"Then I will take away all your treasure."

"You cannot. For my treasure is in heaven and my heart is there."

"Then I will drive you away from every person in the world and you will have no one left."

"No, you cannot. For I have a friend in heaven from whom you cannot separate me."

"Then I will kill you."

"You cannot. Since my life is hidden with Christ in God, I defy you. There is nothing you can do to harm me."

As it was with Nehemiah, so it was with Chrysostom: fear overcoming fears.

Self-promoting fears and self-protecting fears share the prefix *self*. What about me? What about what I want? What about what I need? What about what I deserve? What about what makes me safe? What about what makes me happy? All of these self-centered fears demand that, at the end of the day, you must take care of you and do what's good for you. But Ecclesiastes says that at the end of the day, we are to fear God and obey him. That is the end of the matter and is to be the sum of our lives (Eccl. 12:13).

Why does Ecclesiastes say that? Because it is *Wisdom* Literature. So the end of wisdom is the exact same thing as the beginning of wisdom. The fear of the Lord is the alpha and the omega of wisdom—of Nehemiah's wisdom. We know this not by hearing what he says, but by seeing what he does and how he lives. How will we know this about ourselves? It will not be by what we say. It will be by how we live and what we do, because we will serve, obey, and follow our *true fear*. We will not just proclaim it. We will not just profess it. We will serve it, we will obey it, and we will follow it.

"Relieved." I love Newton's word choice in "Amazing Grace." We do not have these fears because of burdens. The fears *are* the burdens. They are the burdens that grace relieves. God doesn't necessarily relieve *them*; he relieves *us*. And, of course, the irony of our passage is that at the same time that Nehemiah's fears are relieved, his enemies' fears are raised and reinforced. After all of their plotting, scheming, and trying, his adversaries are greatly afraid and humiliated (6:16) as they are confronted with the immovable and insurmountable purposes of God.

The surrounding nations are the victims of their own fears. Unless you fear God, you have to be *afraid* of him. They are not dumb. They know that they have every reason to be afraid. They see the power, but they do not know the grace. And it is only by grace that our fears are relieved. The hymn that Newton wrote is not "Amazing Fear." It is "Amazing Grace."

How Precious Did That Grace Appear . . .

How precious did that grace appear that taught my heart to fear. Even Nehemiah can't just *have* the fear of the Lord. He can't just *do* the fear of the Lord. He can't just apply personal pronouns to the Lord. He is not worthy. He knows this. We hear it from him as he prays in chapter 1 and confesses not just corporate failure, but his own disobedience, corruption, and unworthiness. And yet, in that same prayer, he is bold to ask the God of the covenant promises of steadfast love and redemption to give him grace—grace that takes him from the servile fear of dread and terror that his enemies have to the adoring filial family fear that beloved children have. And though he is right to ask, Nehemiah has no idea what that family grace will ultimately cost. But we do.

What does it cost? The cost is the eternally beloved Son becoming servile and even becoming the enemy as our sin. That Son came in our flesh, living and delighting in the perfect fear of the Lord (Isa. 11:3). That fear took him to a garden that was very different from Eden. He was not there to go running from God in a shattered relationship. He came there running toward his Father, to collapse on him in order to face his fears.

The Gospel writers strain for language to present Jesus's experience in Gethsemane. It's not that it's too strong to say he was fearful. It's not strong enough. We find descriptions of unparalleled distress, of dreadful anguish, of a depth of sorrow that is death itself, of an agony so great that his capillaries burst and bloody sweat actually poured from him. And it was all *rational* fear, that is, *realistic* fear. Those fears were only intensified by the realities he faced in that garden during that divine conversation. That night in Gethsemane is the only occasion when Jesus is said to have fallen prostrate on his face, and as he covered his eyes, he saw nothing but hell yawning before him. Here is the horror of the One who lived wholly for the Father facing complete abandonment by him as he became the very sin that God hates.

And yet, for all of the repeated stress on his agony, the dominant point of each Gospel account is Jesus's resolution to embrace the Father's will. He willingly *gave* his life. No one took it from him. He trusted the Father with all of his heart, even when his heart was broken. So much stronger in him than all that fear was his absolutely submissive love for the Father and his absolutely unstoppable love for us. Those loves overcame what was overwhelming. He embraced it. He went to that cross. He went to that tomb. And we will *never* have to face his fear because his perfect love and what it accomplished for us casts it out (1 John 4:18). Perfect love casts out all of that fear, all of that dread, all of that terror, all of that horror, all of that agony, because he bore every single one of those crushing realities for us. But our Savior's love doesn't just leave us without those fears. The forgiveness won by that love actually wins for us the gift of fear: "With you there is forgiveness, that you may be feared" (Ps. 130:4).

I had the joy of working many years with many college women. Late one night, I received a call from one of them. She came over, and we stayed up into the morning as she blurted out several personal symptoms stemming from crippling fearfulness and anxiety: eating issues, dating disappointments, dread of her upcoming graduation, crushing family expectations. After hours of listening and feeling a growing inadequacy to offer anything specifically helpful, I grabbed her by both shoulders and said, "Honey, do you have any idea how *much* God loves you?" Long pause. Bewildered look. "I guess not," she finally said. "I feel like I'm always on trial for how much I love him."

Perhaps that's where some of you are. I want you to know how much God loves you. The perfect love that casts out our fear can never be *ours* for him, but can only ever be *his* for us. If we belong to him as Nehemiah did, we have the fullness of his love right now. We have the fullness of his grace right now. We have only to dig into what is already there.

A friend's sister bought an apartment in New York City. It had outside space with actual grass in it (about seven square feet). So she and her husband were going to build a new fence so their children could stand there (or whatever they could do in that amount of space). They moved in and were living their dream with the kids out in the "yard." The mom was looking wistfully at them one day when she saw rats out there as well. They had dug under the fence. So the family put the fence deeper into the ground. It took longer, but more rats appeared. They went deeper with the fence. It took a bit longer, but here came the rats. They had to go eighteen feet in the ground to keep out those rats.

We plant our lives in God's grace and think, "That's it, we've arrived." But very soon crushing fears and anxieties come creeping in. What's wrong? If we have the fullness, what's missing? Why are these fears creeping in? We've got to dig deeper into what's *already there*. When we do, it might take longer, but here come the fears and anxieties again, and they're bringing new ones with them.

We've got to dig deeper. Though delayed and in different form, they invade again. We've got to dig deeper. Deeper into that preciousness. Deeper into that grace. Deeper into the bottomless fullness of what is ours in Jesus. We must dig deeper so that the fear of the Lord stands taller and taller in our lives and the anxious fears of our hearts are fenced out and *relieved*. We do not see Nehemiah in chapters 5 and 6 getting braver. We see him digging deeper.

If the fear of the Lord is the beginning and end of wisdom, we could say it's the beginning and end of having sense. But as we've seen, Nehemiah goes against common sense again and again. But his is not *common* sense. That's because it's not *common* fear because it is not taught by *common* grace. It's *miraculous*. Or, to use Newton's word, it's *amazing*. Are we amazed at its preciousness?

'Twas grace that taught my heart to fear. Grace my fears relieved. How precious did that grace appear that won for me the treasure of fear.

Reflect and Pray

Reflect on each question, and then take a moment to speak or write the prayers that grow from those reflections.

1. This talk develops the theme of fearing God. Look back through Nehemiah 5–6 (and even back to chapter 4) and trace the references to fearing God. What do you observe? What phrases stand out? *His fear produced obedience & boldness*

2. What would have been put at risk if Nehemiah had chosen not to fear God and instead to fear his enemies? In light of that, what do you find encouraging in the climax of this section, in Nehemiah 6:15–16?

3. God's people in the church today would seem to have much to fear from those in power and from those in the world around who do not know him. What things do we especially tend to fear, and why? How does God's triumph over his people's enemies through Christ (Col. 2:13–15) give us confidence today to walk in the fear of God?

He shamed them. Publically by victory authentic. He disarmed the spiritual rulers & authorities.

the nation of Israel was His own love

vs. 15 He disarmed the spiritual rulers & authorities.

vs. 14. He cancelled the record of the charges against us and took it away by nailing it to the cross.

Think Like an Expositor

Developing good, effective illustrations can be challenging. We asked Paige Brown to explain how she gathers such amazing stories and how she tells them with her own "Paige-ness" that so genuinely captures audiences.

"I love stories," says Paige. "Narnia resonates with me much more strongly than *Mere Christianity*. And 1 Kings more readily than Galatians. I use analogies and illustrations in conversations with my kids all the time. I kind of think in illustrations."

How does she collect these stories? You can picture it through her answer. "I have scraps of paper and napkins with thoughts of such everywhere when I am preparing because they just come to me," she says. "Ideas don't stick with me unless they get some 'flesh' on them."

But it's not just stories for stories' sake. There's a theological connection to Paige's comments on stories: "I am so grateful that Jesus wasn't just a great preacher, but a master storyteller who 'said nothing to them without a parable' so that the things hidden of old could be made known" (Matt. 13:34–35).

Indeed, it's clear that Paige loves words and the Word—and that she takes time with words in her preparation. She says: "I read the book several times through, and then my assigned chapters several more times before reading anything else. And I noticed something different with each reading. Endless treasures . . ."

4

Coming Together around God's Word

Nehemiah 7–8

Nancy Guthrie

In my years growing up in church, we often sang this chorus:

> The joy of the Lord is my strength.
> The joy of the Lord is my strength.
> The joy of the Lord is my strength.
> The joy of the Lord is my strength.

Simple enough. But as many times as I sang that song, I'm not sure I ever really understood what it meant. Certainly I never knew where it came from in the Bible—in the setting of Nehemiah's day, among God's people who have returned from exile to a broken-down, burned-out city of Jerusalem.

Did you sing this song as a child? Did you think, like I did, that it was all about ha, ha, ha, ha, ha, ha, ha happiness? Maybe we should figure out what this joy is and how it can strengthen us as the people of God as we live in a world in which so many things threaten our joy and sap our strength.

Now, I think I know what joy is in general—or at least I know what it is to want to be happy. I've chased after all kinds of things that I thought would make me happy. Perhaps it started for me with chasing boys on the playground at David Brewer Elementary School. Many a young girl, at one time or another, has entertained the thought that if only she could catch the right boy, *then* she would be happy! Some of us have chased after a particular position in a particular company or organization that we thought would make us happy, only to discover that we were thrown in with co-workers, bosses, or leaders who made us crazy instead of happy. Others of us have thought that if we could just create the family of our dreams—made up of just the right number of healthy children who would never squabble, but would beg for family devotions to begin—*then* we'd be happy. Still others of us have thought that if we could attain a certain number on the scale, a certain level of accomplishment, or a certain place in our community, *then* we'd be happy.

Clearly, we need something more solid and durable than the fleeting happiness we've been able to generate. And it seems that something more is being described here by Nehemiah. This is not merely a joy that you and I can create for ourselves or for each other. This is the joy of the Lord, or *the Lord's* joy. The Lord intends for *his* joy to be *our* joy (John 15:11).

So what is the joy of *the Lord*? In what way was the joy of the Lord—God's very own joy—the strength of the returned exiles in the city of Jerusalem in Nehemiah's day? And what would it mean for this same joy—the joy of the Lord—to be *our strength* as we live out our days—not ensconced within the rebuilt walls of Jerusalem, but wherever we call home?

Before the events of Nehemiah, when these people were living in exile, the psalmist says they sat down and wept by the waters of Babylon when their captors wanted them to sing songs of Zion. "How shall we sing the LORD's song in a foreign land?" they asked. "If I forget you, O Jerusalem, let my right hand forget its skill! Let my tongue stick to the roof of my mouth, if I do not remember you, if I do not set Jerusalem above my highest joy!" (Ps. 137:4–6). The highest joy for the people of God was and is to be at home in God's city. And that is God's joy as well. It's the first answer to our pursuit of discovering from Nehemiah 7–8 what the joy of the Lord is.

The Lord's Joy Is Bringing His People into the Security of His City

> Now when the wall had been built and I had set up the doors, and the gatekeepers, the singers, and the Levites had been appointed, I gave my brother Hanani and Hananiah the governor of the castle charge over Jerusalem, for he was a more faithful and God-fearing man than many. And I said to them, "Let not the gates of Jerusalem be opened until the sun is hot. And while they are still standing guard, let them shut and bar the doors. Appoint guards from among the inhabitants of Jerusalem, some at their guard posts and some in front of their own homes." The city was wide and large, but the people within it were few, and no houses had been rebuilt. (Neh. 7:1–4)

Jerusalem must have still looked much like the war-torn, bombed-out cities we see on the news today, with piles of rubble where there were once homes—not exactly the neighborhood anyone wants to move into with their kids. It was a city on a hill with no wall, which made it a very dangerous place to live. So when the exiles returned home, though their hearts had longed for Jerusalem, most didn't move back in, but instead settled in towns and villages surrounding the city. In Nehemiah's day, only a few brave souls were actually living in the city of Jerusalem.

But this was to be a place where God's people could dwell in peace, worshiping him and shining as a light to the Gentiles.

So Nehemiah began taking steps to secure the city so that God's people could live there. He put in charge his brother Hanani, who cared enough about the city to make the four-month-long journey to Susa to tell Nehemiah about its great trouble and great shame (Neh. 1:1–3), along with Hananiah, the governor appointed by the Persian ruler, who evidently feared God more than he feared man. Guards were set at the gates to ensure security for those who lived inside. The intention of Nehemiah and ultimately God's joyful purpose was that those who lived in his city would dwell secure.

But that did raise a question: *Who* should live in the Lord's city, within those rebuilt walls? *Who* should populate this city that was at the center of God's salvation purposes in the world?

> Then my God put it into my heart to assemble the nobles and the officials and the people to be enrolled by genealogy. And I found the book of the genealogy of those who came up at the first, and I found written in it:
> These were the people of the province who came up out of the captivity of those exiles whom Nebuchadnezzar the king of Babylon had carried into exile. They returned to Jerusalem and Judah, each to his town. They came with Zerubbabel, Jeshua, Nehemiah, Azariah, Raamiah, Nahamani, Mordecai, Bilshan, Mispereth, Bigvai, Nehum, Baanah. (Neh. 7:5–7a)

If you are rebuilding a city, but more than that, if you are restoring a people to live in that city, a people who will worship God in the way in which he is worthy to be worshiped, where do you begin in determining who will populate the city? Nehemiah began by pulling out the list of families who were the first to return to Judah when the doors were thrown open. We read about them in Ezra 1:5: "Then rose up the heads of the fathers' houses of Judah and Benjamin, and the priests and the Levites, _everyone whose spirit God had stirred_ to go up to rebuild the house of the LORD that is in Jerusalem." The reality was that returning to the Jewish homeland wasn't all that tempting to most Judeans who had settled down to a new life in exile. But there were some whose spirits God had stirred up to go back. Nehemiah intended for Jerusalem to be inhabited by those whose hearts burned for the city of God because the Spirit of God had kindled that fire within them.

In chapter 7, we see that Nehemiah listed the people who made their way back from exile to Judah ninety years earlier. First, in verses 8–38, we have the list of ordinary citizens; then, in 39–42, the list of priests; in 43–45, the list of Levites, including the singers; then, in 46–65, the list of the temple servants and Solomon's servants, as well as those who claimed citizenship and membership in the priesthood but didn't have the records to demonstrate it.

This list of difficult-to-pronounce names takes me back to my childhood, when I got the unfortunate assignment of reading long passages of names in Sunday school. The truth is, when we come to lists of names like this one, we're tempted to think the names don't really matter.

Oh, but they do.

If we had started at the beginning of God's story of redemption in the Old Testament, surely some of these names would ring some bells for us. We would recognize that these were the descendants of Abraham, to whom God promised to give this land. These were members of the nation God brought out of slavery to live in this land of milk and honey. These were the descendants of those God drove out of his land because of their spiritual adultery and disobedience—with the promise that they would one day be replanted in the land. Most significantly, these were the people from whom the Promised One was going to come—the descendant of Abraham through whom all of the families of the earth would be blessed.

These returnees, mostly of the tribes of Judah and Benjamin, were the people of God, the heirs of the promises made to their forefathers. Nehemiah made a list of the leaders, and there were twelve of them (v. 7). Just as God's people were once led by the twelve sons of Jacob, and just as God's people would be led in the future by the twelve apostles, here in Nehemiah we are signaled that these were now the people of God by the record that they were led by twelve men whose spirits God had stirred to go up to rebuild the house of the Lord in Jerusalem.

We also know there were those in this group who were *not* descendants of Abraham, but had joined themselves to the people of God because they wanted in on the promises of God. Ezra 6 describes those who celebrated the first Passover in the land, saying that "it was eaten by the people of Israel who had returned from exile, *and also by every one who had joined them and separated himself from the uncleanness of the peoples of the land to worship the* Lord, *the God of Israel*" (v. 21). Just as we know that some Egyptians joined God's people who walked out of Egypt, and just as we know that Canaanites and Moabites such as Rahab and Ruth became a part of God's people by forsaking their false gods and worshiping Yahweh alone, we see that in Nehemiah's day, God was adding people from throughout the lands conquered by the Persians. God has always been and always will be about the work of bringing people from every tribe, tongue, and nation to himself.

Aren't we grateful to know that we who were "alienated from the commonwealth of Israel and strangers to the covenants of promise, having no hope and without God in the world" (Eph. 2:12), are now "no longer strangers and aliens, but . . . fellow citizens with the saints and members of the household of God" (v. 19)? Aren't we grateful to know that our names are included in the list of those whom God's spirit has stirred up to walk away from the Babylon called "this world" so that we might enter into the city of God and find our security there?

Here is the joy of the Lord that can be your joy as you read this long list of unpronounceable names: God's people are not nameless, faceless people to him.

The Lord's Joy Is Recording the Names of His People in His Book

God likes to keep lists of those who are his people because his people as a group matter to him, his people as families matter to him, and his people as individuals matter to him.[1] Their names are written in his "book." We read about this book throughout Scripture. The first place we see it mentioned is in Exodus, when Moses was willing for his name to be blotted out of the Lord's book in exchange for forgiveness for his people (32:32). The psalmist writes about the Lord's book, in which the names of those "enrolled among the righteous" are found (69:28). The prophet Daniel writes that God's people will be delivered. And who will those people be? "Everyone whose name shall be found written in the book" (Dan. 12:1).

Jesus said, "Rejoice that your names are written in heaven" (Luke 10:20). Here is joy that gives us strength—the joy that the Lord takes in writing our names in his book as those who will live securely in his city, the New Jerusalem, with him forever. Knowing that our names are written in heaven strengthens us for living life on this earth. We can face disappointment and disaster, and ultimately we can face death strengthened in the knowledge that our lives cannot be ruined, they cannot be snuffed out. Our names will not be, cannot be, blotted out from God's book.

"So the priests, the Levites, the gatekeepers, the singers, some of the people, the temple servants, and all Israel, lived in their towns. And when the seventh month had come, the people of Israel were in their towns" (Neh. 7:73). You and I tend to read right through this time-stamp of "the seventh month" because we don't immediately grasp the significance of it. But just as every seventh day was holy to the Lord for Sabbath rest (Ex. 20:8–10), and just as every seventh year was holy under Mosaic law so that the land—the ground—was given a "Sabbath of solemn rest" (Lev. 25:4–5),

---

[1] Adapted from a statement by Kevin DeYoung in his sermon on Ezra 2, "A Particular People," given at University Reformed Church, East Lansing, Michigan, on January 29, 2012.

so the seventh month was set apart as something special. Back in Leviticus 23, we read that "the LORD spoke to Moses, saying, 'Speak to the people of Israel, saying, In the seventh month, on the first day of the month, you shall observe a day of solemn rest, a memorial proclaimed with blast of trumpets, a holy convocation'" (vv. 23–24). A holy convocation—that's what's happening when we read, "And all the people gathered as one man into the square before the Water Gate" (Neh. 8:1a).

All of these people, who were living in their towns surrounding Jerusalem, converged into the city. We might think they came to the temple, but that's not the case. Women were limited to the outer courts, and only priests could enter the innermost areas of the temple. But here were gathered, according to verse 2, "both men and women and all who could understand what they heard." Fifty thousand people gathered at the busiest intersection in the city, the place where people would go in and out of the city to get water. Perhaps it looked something like the crowds of people who converge into Times Square in New York City on New Year's Eve. But these people were not gathered to watch a ball drop. They gathered to hear a book read. They gathered to rediscover and recapture their identity as the people of God. They gathered "as one man," meaning that they had a unified desire: they wanted to hear God speak to them through his written Word.

"And they told Ezra the scribe to bring the Book of the Law of Moses that the LORD had commanded Israel" (Neh. 8:1b). Imagine what it might have been like in that square on that day. Perhaps a few people scattered throughout the crowd began to call out, "Bring out the book!" Then a few more joined in, calling out to Ezra, "Bring out the book!" until fifty thousand voices strong they thundered, "*Bring out the book!*"

Most people today would scoff at the idea that the central source in which to discover the reality of who you are, of who you were created to be, and of what you are meant to do could be the pages of an ancient book. Maybe we presume that idea would have been more believable in Nehemiah's day. But consider that when the events we are reading about took place, the Book of the Law of Moses was already an ancient book. It was already a thousand years old. And consider that these were people who had never heard the voice of God speaking to them from a mountain that was on fire, as their ancestors did at Sinai (Exodus 19). They'd never seen a cloud of fire hovering over the temple to signify God's presence among them, as their ancestors did in Solomon's day (2 Chron. 7:1–3). But they did want to hear from God in their day. So how would that happen? And how can we expect to hear God speaking to us in our day when we've never heard an audible voice from heaven or had a supernatural experience? God speaks to us, revealing to us who he is and what he has done, helping us understand who we are in relationship to him, through his written Word.

The people gathered at the gate were not hungry for some sort of spiritual experience apart from God's Word. They were not heading out to find places to be alone, where they might silence themselves and listen to hear a special word all about them spoken into their private thoughts. They were hungry to hear God speaking to them in such a way that they would know for sure it was his voice they were hearing.

Oh, that God might raise up men and women in our day who are hungry for the book—hungrier for the book than we are for an inspirational or entertaining experience, hungrier for the book than we are for Pinterest-worthy aesthetics, hungrier for the book than for good advice to solve what we see as our most significant problems; hungry to hear God's voice break through the busyness of raising children, the ding of another email message arriving, the draw of popular bloggers; willing to let God set the agenda of the conversation; open to what he says even if it doesn't sit well; invested in growing in a right understanding; convinced that what he says is the truest truth, the most solid foundation, the most nourishing food; and certain that his promises are our surest expectation and that obeying his commands will generate our deepest joys.

"And he read from it facing the square before the Water Gate from early morning until midday, in the presence of the men and the women and those who could understand. And the ears of all the people were attentive to the Book of the Law" (Neh. 8:3). They not only *asked* for the book, they were *attentive* to it. They didn't merely go through the motions of showing up while their thoughts were elsewhere (which, can we admit, is often the case for us when we gather to hear the Word read and taught?). They were taking in God's Word, thinking it through, seeking to understand and apply it.

Here's the picture: Ezra is standing on a wooden platform that they had built for just this purpose. This is not a spontaneous gathering; it has been planned and prepared for. Ezra opens up the book—the scrolls—of Genesis, Exodus, Leviticus, Numbers, and Deuteronomy, and he begins to read. From dawn until about noon, the people listen to Ezra read. They haven't come to hear Ezra's ideas or Nehemiah's plans. They've come to hear the living God speak to them through his written Word, so they stand to receive it (vv. 4–5).

"And Ezra blessed the LORD, the great God, and all the people answered, 'Amen, Amen,' lifting up their hands. And they bowed their heads and worshiped the LORD with their faces to the ground" (v. 6). They were not just listening politely or passively. Their posture was a reflection of what was happening in their hearts as they opened themselves to welcome, affirm, and submit to all that God had to say to them. Ezra was surrounded by the Levites, who, according to verses 7–8, "helped the people understand the Law, while the people remained in their places. They read from the book, from the Law of God, clearly, and they gave the sense, so that the people understood the reading."

Perhaps Ezra read from Genesis about the curse, and the promise in the midst of the curse, of the Seed of the woman who would crush the head of the Serpent. And the Levites worked their way through groups of people in the large gathering, explaining what it meant—how the curse explains why the world doesn't work right, and how humanity began to wait for the baby to be born, this One who would put an end to the curse. Perhaps Ezra read to them about the Tower of Babel and the confusion of languages. Most of these people likely spoke Aramaic and no longer understood Hebrew. But as the Levites translated and explained God's Word to them, they began to understand that God would not allow the effects of Babel to keep his people from hearing and understanding his Word.

The Joy of the Lord Is His People Hearing and Understanding His Word

The deeper your understanding of God's Word goes, the more his Word becomes interwoven into the fabric of your life and the more you experience his strength. Just as the man who built his house upon the rock by working the Word into his life was strengthened so that when the storm came, his house did not fall (Matt. 7:25), you will be strengthened to face the inevitable storms of life as you hear, understand, and live in light of God's Word.

As the people of God gathered at the Water Gate that day heard and understood God's Word, they took in the promises God had made to Abraham of a great name, a great nation, and a vast land, as well as a promise that through his descendants all the families of the earth would be blessed. They heard how Abraham's family became a nation in captivity in Egypt and how God sent a deliverer to redeem them from slavery. How they must have groaned when Ezra read about their nation's disobedience in the wilderness. As they listened to God speaking through Moses in Deuteronomy, promising them blessing if they would obey and curses if they disobeyed, surely they understood that their forefathers had experienced all of the curses warned about in the ancient book. In response, Nehemiah tells us, "all the people wept" (8:9).

Some people hear the Word of God read and explained but feel nothing. They have a hardness toward it, a lack of response to it. But not on this day; not these people. As they took in all that God had done for them, all of the promises he had made to them, all that he had commanded them to do and be, and all of the patience he had shown, it penetrated them so deeply that they were moved to tears. The Word of God, the book of Hebrews tells us, is "sharper than any two-edged sword, piercing to the division of soul and of spirit, of joints and of marrow, and discerning the thoughts and intentions of the heart" (4:12). Clearly it cut deeply into the hearts of the people gathered that day, exposing all of the ways they had fallen short of the glory of God. They saw the incongruity of their lives in relation to God's law, along with their lack of gratitude for God's provision, and they wept.

Tears began to trickle down their faces as they heard about, understood, and felt the weight of the failure of God's people over the centuries to be all they were intended to be. Certainly this record of rebellion and their growing awareness of the reality of their own spiritual condition were worthy of weeping over. And the time was coming for tears of repentance, but this was not the time.

"And Nehemiah, who was the governor, and Ezra the priest and scribe, and the Levites who taught the people said to all the people, 'This day is holy to the LORD your God; do not mourn or weep.' For all the people wept as they heard the words of the Law" (Neh. 8:9). While those gathered at the Water Gate that day heard of the repeated disobedience and failure of the people of God throughout the centuries, that's not all they heard. They heard about God's provision of a way to be forgiven, a way to be cleansed, a way to experience, at least in part, the restoration of the full relationship God had begun working out long before in the garden. They saw in shadows the Redeemer who would accomplish this full restoration.

As Ezra read the Law of Moses and the Levites moved through

the crowd to explain it, the people understood the significance of so much in their lives that had devolved into meaningless religious ritual. From Genesis, they would have heard how God provided a substitute, a ram caught in a thicket, so that Abraham did not have to sacrifice his beloved son. When Ezra got to Exodus, they would have learned how God made provision for a lamb to be sacrificed for every household on Passover night in place of the firstborn. And when Ezra got to Leviticus, they would have heard God's instructions for the Day of Atonement, when a single animal was sacrificed for the sins of the whole nation of Israel. It was pictured for them again and again—that someone can be made right with God only on the basis of the lamb God has provided. They couldn't clearly see the perfect Lamb God was going to provide, but as they heard and understood the Book of the Law as Ezra read it, it nurtured in them a longing for "the Lamb of God who takes away the sin of the world!" (John 1:29).

When we hear God's Word read and taught, it does much more than reveal our sin; it reveals our Savior. God's good word to his people is that our sin will not get the final word in our lives. His grace and mercy will get the final word. The joy of the Lord is this word of grace toward sinners, which you and I can understand even better than the people of Nehemiah's day, because we live on this side of the cross and can read and understand the complete Old and New Testaments. Because of grace, when we hear and understand God's Word, we are not left to simmer in a pool of regret and shame. Sorrow over sin must give way to joy. Knowing that it is the Lord's joy to extend grace to sinners gives us strength to live for him and love him rather than run from him.

Ezra and Nehemiah wanted the wonder of God's saving purposes for his people, his patience toward them, his presence with them, his provision for them, and his continued promises to them to prompt celebration, not tears. Ezra and Nehemiah instructed the people to celebrate with a feast, saying: "Go your way. Eat the fat and drink sweet wine and send portions to anyone who has nothing ready, for this day is holy to our Lord. And do not be grieved, for the joy of the LORD is your strength" (Neh. 8:10).

This command to feast didn't come from out of the blue. The people had heard Ezra read about God setting out a feast for Adam and Eve of the fruit of every tree but one. Of course, instead of eating what God commanded them to eat, Adam and Eve took and ate what they were commanded not to eat. In this way, they brought judgment upon themselves and all who would come after them. But as the people gathered at the Water Gate continued to listen, they learned that the way back into fellowship with God was to worship him by taking and eating of his provision. As Ezra read Numbers, they heard of a table that God spread for his people in the wilderness, raining down manna and bringing water out of a rock. They heard his command to worship and commune with him by partaking of his feasts and festivals outlined in Leviticus. They began to understand that the feasts God had instructed them to celebrate weren't empty traditions or meaningless ceremonies, but that every invitation to eat and drink at God's table was a welcome back into fellowship with him. And they wanted in!

"And all the people went their way to eat and drink and to send portions and to make great rejoicing, because they had understood the words that were declared to them" (Neh. 8:12). Great rejoicing!

The Joy of the Lord Is His People Partaking of His Feast

To eat the fat and drink sweet wine was a tangible way of partaking of the grace of God, his promised provision. It demonstrated trust in his ultimate provision, which was made manifest when, "on the night when he was betrayed [Jesus] took bread, and when he had given thanks, he broke it, and said, 'This is my body which is for you. Do this in remembrance of me.' In the same way also he took the cup, after supper, saying, 'This cup is the new covenant in my blood. Do this, as often as you drink it, in remembrance of me'" (1 Cor. 11:23–25).

Week after week, as we gather as God's people, and the Word of God is read and we're given the sense of it so that we understand it, we rightly feel the weight of our failure to be all that God has intended for us to be. But he does not send us away in sorrow. Instead, we are invited to his table, where we feast on his broken body and his shed blood, so that we leave with great rejoicing. We find that partaking in *the Lord's feast* fills us with *the Lord's joy*. This joy gives us strength to believe that our sins have been fully and finally dealt with in the sacrifice of Christ. It strengthens us to live lives that reflect the holiness of our God. It strengthens us to share the provision of God with those who have none. We simply can't fill ourselves up with the feast provided for us in the person and work of Christ and keep it to ourselves. We have to share it so that the joy of the Lord—this salvation feast—will become their strength too.

> On the second day the heads of fathers' houses of all the people, with the priests and the Levites, came together to Ezra the scribe in order to study the words of the Law. And they found it written in the Law that the LORD had commanded by Moses that the people of Israel should dwell in booths during the feast of the seventh month. (Neh. 8:13–14)

It was not just a wall or an ancient city that was being restored in Jerusalem. The people of God were being restored—families who needed dads to lead in living out God's gracious law. So the men came to immerse themselves in God's book. As they studied, they discovered that God required something they and their ancestors had not been doing, or had been doing in only a token way, for centuries. On the fifteenth day of the seventh month, they were to make booths out of branches and live outdoors in them for a week. As they slept outside in their makeshift shelters, they would be reminded of God's provision for their ancestors when they wandered in the wilderness for forty years after being released from their slavery. They would be reminded that they, too, had been released from their exile and brought back by God's good hand. They would be reminded that they were, in fact, still pilgrim people in the world, dependent upon God's provision and presence, even though they were back living in the land. We read in verse 16, "So the people went out and brought [branches] and made booths for themselves." They read in the Law of God that they should do it, and then they went home, gathered their families together, and said, "We're going to obey God."

How many times have we read something in the Bible or had the Word taught clearly to us, showing us something we ought to do, and thought, "Yeah, I should do that." But then we sang the closing hymn, walked away, and put it out of our minds, more concerned about what we were going to eat for lunch. What happened in Jerusalem was completely different. They read about the forgotten Festival of Tabernacles and they immediately made booths for themselves and lived in them for seven days.

And did this obedience make them miserable? Not at all. "And there was very great rejoicing" (v. 17). There it is again—joy.

The Joy of the Lord Is His People Living in Glad Obedience to His Word

Have you discovered this joy of the Lord? Have you discovered that saying yes to God's commands actually brings you greater joy than whatever it is that tempts you to ignore or defy what God has commanded? That's how it was for the people in Nehemiah's day. The Festival of Tabernacles pointed *back* to that time in the desert when God's presence was manifest among his people in the center of their camp in the form of a pillar of cloud by day and a pillar of fire by night. They considered God's gracious presence among his people in the past and felt joy. The Festival of Tabernacles also pointed *forward* to the day John described when he wrote, "The Word became human and made his home among us" (John 1:14 NLT). They anticipated that day when God's presence would be manifest among his people in flesh and blood, and it gave them joy.

The day is coming when we will experience all that was celebrated in the Festival of Tabernacles. We'll finally live in our forever home, where we will enjoy the presence of God in our midst. We'll remember how he rescued us from the land of our slavery to sin and brought us out of the wilderness of this world into the safety and security of our eternal home. And there will be very great rejoicing—outrageous, overflowing, unending joy!

It is the Lord's joy to bring his people into the security of his city. Just as Nehemiah set guards at the gates of Jerusalem, God has set his guard at his gate. In fact, Jesus is not only the one who stands guard at the gate; Jesus *is* the gate (John 10:7). He is the way by which we enter the city of God (John 14:6). And, oh, the safety you and I enjoy because of Christ! He says about those who have come into the safety of his fold, the Lord's city, "I give them eternal life, and they will never perish, and no one will snatch them out of my hand" (John 10:28).

Oh, the joy of putting down roots and making our home in the city of God, knowing we're safe from the enemy of our souls and protected from the wrath we deserve—that is the joy that gives us strength. It gives us the strength we need to live as aliens and strangers in the city of man, free from fear about the future. We don't have to live in fear of the impact of the national debt or the nuclear threat. We don't have to be afraid of a natural disaster or a terminal diagnosis. "Though our outer self is wasting away, our inner self is being renewed day by day. For this light momentary affliction is preparing for us an eternal weight of glory beyond all comparison" (2 Cor. 4:16–17).

One day, we will be welcomed into the New Jerusalem, which is surrounded by "a great, high wall, with twelve gates." The walls of this city will be "built of jasper." The foundations of the wall of the city will be adorned with every kind of jewel (Rev. 21:12–21). Unlike the gates of Jerusalem in Nehemiah's day, which were shut and barred to keep her enemies out, the gates of the New Jerusalem will never be shut (v. 25). Yet nothing unclean will ever enter that city (v. 27). Don't you long for the day when you will enter into the complete security of the Lord's city? Is your confident expectation of this glorious future bringing you joy now?

It is the Lord's joy to record the names of his people in his book. In Revelation 21, John tells us, "Only those who are written in the Lamb's book of life" will populate the New Jerusalem (v. 27). Entrance into that city will not be based on the blood coursing through our veins, but on the blood of the Lamb, which has covered and cleansed away our sin. We will not be bored when that list of names is read! We'll be on pins and needles listening for our names. What joy we will experience on that day when our names are found written in the book of life! The psalmist wrote, "All the days ordained for me were written in your book before one of them came to be" (Ps. 139:16 NIV). The joy of having our *names* recorded in his book strengthens us to face every *day* written in his book—especially the day the accident happens, the day we get the diagnosis, the day our dream dies.

It is the Lord's joy for his people to hear, understand, and obey his Word. Oh, the joy of that day when everything Ezra read about from the Book of the Law will come to its consummation. The Seed of the woman will have destroyed the Serpent. The people of God will have come through the wilderness of this world and into the true Promised Land. All who were once unclean and have now been made clean by the blood of an all-sufficient sacrifice will, on that day, be made holy to live in God's presence in the ultimate Most Holy Place called the new heaven and new earth. On that day, not just fifty thousand people, but a great multitude, and not just descendants of Abraham, but people from every nation, tribe, and tongue, will stand, not at the Water Gate, but around the throne, crying out with a loud voice, "Salvation belongs to our God who sits on the throne, and to the Lamb!" (Rev. 7:10). We'll gather around God's Word, which we will hear, not read by Ezra, but spoken by the very mouth of God. We'll hear with our ears a loud voice from the throne, saying: "Behold, the dwelling place of God is with man. He will dwell with them, and they will be his people, and God himself will be with them as their God" (Rev. 21:3). Everything the Festival of Tabernacles was intended to picture and promise will have become the reality we will live in forever. This promise—a promise that brings the Lord great joy—provides you and me with the strength we need to live now in light of that coming day.

/ *It is the Lord's joy for his people to partake of his feast.* As we enter into the New Jerusalem that day, we'll be invited to sit down to eat the fat and drink sweet wine. Together we'll cry out: "Hallelujah! For the Lord our God the Almighty reigns. Let us rejoice and exult and give him the glory, for the marriage of the Lamb has come" (Rev. 19:6–7).

Why would we settle for the happiness the world offers when we are being invited into the joy of the Lord? Why would we ever search for the happiness our hearts long for anywhere other than in "the city that has foundations, whose designer and builder is God" (Heb. 11:10)? There we will come under the security of his protection. There we will be counted among his people, finding our names written in his book. There we will hear his voice like never before, understand his Word like never before, and serve him in glad obedience like never before. There we will partake of his feast to our full and unending satisfaction.

Reflect and Pray

Reflect on each question, and then take a moment to speak or write the prayers that grow from those reflections.

1. You probably didn't memorize any part of Nehemiah 7 as a child in Sunday school. And yet, Nancy Guthrie shows us the beauty of God's personal care for his people and of the fact that he knows us by name and records our names in his book. What difference does it make to you that our Shepherd knows his sheep by name (John 10:3)?

   It is Comforting. It is Security — Eternal Security

2. As God's people gathered, they listened attentively to God's Word and to God's servants, the Levites, who helped them understand. Trace that word *understand* through Nehemiah 8. In what ways do you struggle sometimes with understanding God's Word? What encouragements do you find here? *Its possible for all to understand we need to get help at times. Its*

3. Nancy points out several themes woven throughout the *worth* Bible that appear in this passage—like the secure city with *at* walls, the feasting, and God's desire to dwell among his *under* people—and shows how these themes will reach their *stand* fullness in the new heaven and new earth, our everlasting home. What are several ways this sure hope of enduring fellowship with God through Christ can strengthen you today, in the midst of all that you face? *He is with me*

He is joy & that gives me strength

Think Like an Expositor *He will give me his strength*

What do you do when you first take up a text that you will teach or lead others in understanding? Nancy offered a lively description of her initial process of observation and asking questions:

First, I read through the entire book of Nehemiah to get a sense of the story and how these two chapters fit into the whole. Then I printed out the text of the two chapters with lots of space and began to mark it up, noting words, jotting notes and questions within the text. And I had *lots* of questions. Why were there so few people living in Jerusalem? Why did Nehemiah look for the book with the list of the exiles who had returned many years before? Why are we given the name and numeric detail? Why did some people claim to be on the list, but their names weren't found? What was the significance of the seventh month? Why did they gather at the Water Gate? What might this scene have looked like with the Levites "giving the sense" of what Ezra read? What was the joy of the Lord that would be their strength? What was the meaning of the Feast of Tabernacles? I began to search out answers to these questions by reading commentaries, listening to audio of sound teachers, and asking people who know more about the Bible than I do.

One of the most helpful things I did was to take the printed-out text and my list of questions and sit down with someone who loves God's Word, knows Hebrew, and gets as excited as I do about figuring out how to communicate the Scriptures rightly, David Filson. I was able to ask him things like: *Was this book originally written in Hebrew or Aramaic? Is it a stretch to suggest from 7:12 that Zerubbabel and the eleven with him represent the new people of God? Why aren't trumpets mentioned if this is the time of the Feast of Trumpets (the first day of the seventh month)? Why isn't the Day of Atonement here in chapter 8? Does that mean they didn't observe it? How do I reconcile Ezra 3:4 with Nehemiah 8:17?* We spent two hours just talking through the text, exploring the history and setting, the drama and emotion, what was there as well as what wasn't there, the implications and possible applications that could be made from it.

Nancy obviously takes joy in connecting this part of the story to many whole-Bible themes and trajectories. Clearly Nehemiah played a crucial role in restoring the nation from which would come the promised Christ and in reinstituting the sacrificial system that pictured and pointed to the saving sacrifice of Christ on the cross. Through this history of redemption wind many themes that unify and reach to the very end. Nancy comments:

There are so many elements in these two chapters that we see again and again from the beginning to the end of Scripture—a city with walls, names written in a book, God's Word going out, feasting, God's desire to dwell among his people. And whenever we see one of these themes within a passage we're preparing to teach, I think we miss out on getting to the real meaning and appropriate application if we don't explore how it connects to the theme throughout the Bible. Connecting to these larger themes helps us stay on track in showing how the text is about God's outworking of his plan to redeem all things through Christ, rather than moving too quickly to individualized or overly simplified applications. To me, it was significant that all of these themes find resolution in part now as we are joined to Christ, but in fullness on that day when Christ returns and establishes the new heaven and new earth.

Since I didn't grow up understanding how to trace these themes, and I didn't grow up with a sense of the trajectory of the Bible's story headed toward restoration, consummation, God dwelling on a redeemed earth with a resurrected people, I assume that many of those I'm teaching haven't either. So I think it is helpful to have those things drawn out, and even essential to grasping the true meaning of this Old Testament text for us as believers today.

5

Responding to God according to His Word

Nehemiah 9–10

John Piper

One of the main lessons from Nehemiah 9 and 10—indeed, from all the Bible—is that God does not exist for the sake of our enjoying biblical stories; biblical stories exist for the sake of our enjoying God.

The reason I make a point of this is not only because it stands out amazingly in Nehemiah 9, but also because in our time there is great fascination with tracing out the storyline of the Bible. I simply want to wave a flag over all this fascination with story and narrative to say: there is a point to the story; there is a point to the narrative—and the point is a person.

Biblical stories are no more ends in themselves than history is an end in itself or the universe is an end in itself. The universe is telling the glory of God (Ps. 19:1). And the history of the world is what it is to show that God is who he is. God writes the story of history to reveal who he is—what he is like, his character, his name.

Consider Nehemiah 9:10. The Levites are praying: "[You] performed signs and wonders against Pharaoh and all his servants and all the people of his land, for you knew that they acted arrogantly against our fathers. *And you made a name for yourself, as it is to this day.*"

What was God doing as he brought ten plagues on Egypt, split the Red Sea, and delivered the people of Israel from bondage? What was he doing as he acted the story that would be told ten thousand times? The answer is at the end of verse 10: he was *making a name for himself.*

Then notice these key words at the end of the verse: "as it is to this day." What day? The day of Nehemiah—about 400 BC. When was God making this name for himself? At the exodus, about 1400 BC—one thousand years earlier!

What is the point of history? God is making a name for himself—a name that will last a thousand years. God is making a name for himself that his people can know, bank on, and exult in for thousands of years. A name—a character, a revelation of who he is and what he is like—so that we can know him, trust him, and enjoy him. That's why there are stories in the Bible.

And that is why I am offering this chapter. I want you to know him. I want you to enjoy him. Some of you know him deeply and have enjoyed his fellowship for many years. Others of you know *about* him. You know some of his rules. You know Christian activities like Bible reading, praying, and church life. But God is not a precious, personal, cherished treasure to you. I would like that to change, as you take in God's powerful Word through the book of Nehemiah.

So now you have the big picture and the big goal: the universe exists, history exists, biblical stories exist, and Nehemiah 9 and 10 exist so that you might meet the living God, and know him and enjoy him. Now let's get more specific.

Seeking the Help of God

After the Feast of Booths in Nehemiah 8—when joy was over-flowing—the time had come for sorrow, fasting, and sackcloth, and for crying out to God for deliverance from the great distress of the people of Israel in Jerusalem. The situation is described in Nehemiah 9:36–37:

> Behold, we are slaves this day; in the land that you gave to our fathers to enjoy its fruit and its good gifts, behold, we are slaves. And its rich yield goes to the kings whom you have set over us because of our sins. They rule over our bodies and over our livestock as they please, and we are in great distress.

That is the situation that precipitates the fasting, sackcloth, and crying out to God that we find in Nehemiah 9, and the covenant they make with God in chapter 10. They sum it up with the words at the end of verse 37: "we are in great distress."

My assumption is that hundreds of you are reading this chapter with those very words like a tightening strap around your soul: "I am in great distress. My marriage . . . my children . . . my church . . . my friendships . . . my soul. Any rest, any joy, fits only into the small spaces between the sorrows of my life."

So, if that's you—and if it's not, it will be—listen with all your heart to how these Levites seek the help of God. Let's start at verse 5: "Then the Levites [these are the assistants to the priests, all from the tribe of Levi], Jeshua, Kadmiel, Bani, Hashabneiah, Sherebiah, Hodiah, Shebaniah, and Pethahiah, said . . . ," and from there to the end of verse 37, they are crying out to God. The words *you* or *your* in reference to God occur thirty times in these verses.

This is what you do when you are in great distress. This is what Israel has always done and what Christians have always done—and what I always do when I am in great distress. But let's make sure we are really clear about their distress before we look at how they pray.

They are not just in distress. They are in distress because of their own sin. And the distress that they are in is distress that God himself has sent upon them. Look again at verse 37: "And its rich yield [that of the land God gave to their fathers!] goes to the kings whom *you have set over us* because of *our sins.* They rule over our bodies and over our livestock as they please, and we are in great distress." God has set slavemasters over them! Because of their sin! So these people are crying for deliverance from a distress that they *deserve* to be in because they have sinned against God, and that God *himself* has put them in because of their sin.

No one reading this should dare to say, "Well, the rest of you can cry out to God for rescue from your distress, but not me, because I have sinned my way into my distress and God himself has appointed my misery." No. You may not say that, because this cry to God that we are about to look at is being lifted up from people just like you. They *do* deserve to be in their distress. And God is the one who sent it on them.

So the question to be asked is clearer now: How do you cry out to God from *that* distress?

Remembering the Story of Salvation

The answer the Levites give is to pray back to God the story that God himself has acted in the history of Israel. They virtually summarize the whole Old Testament in one prayer, from verses 6 to 31. Why do they do that? They do it because they know that God does not exist for the sake of their enjoying the story of the Old Testament; the story exists for the sake of their enjoying God. In other words, they know that God never acts willy-nilly in history. He acts to make a name for himself—to make known his character, his nature, himself. He *does* things a certain way because he *is* a certain way.

These distressed, guilty, God-oppressed Israelites desperately need to see that the God of this Old Testament story is the kind of God who might be willing to rescue them from *their* own sin and *his* own judgment. Is that the kind of God who rules the world? Or not? They know that God has created this story—this history—to make the answer to that question plain.

In verses 6 through 15, the Levites celebrate the greatness of God's power, righteousness, and covenant-keeping salvation. Verse 6a: "You are the LORD, you alone." That is, "You are Yahweh—the God who exists without dependence and without competitor to your being. You have always been. You absolutely are. You say, 'I am who I am' (Ex. 3:14). And there is no other who has absolute being." Here is the great starting point for all of us when we are dealing with the living God—a reverential, humble, glad recognition that we are dependent, God is independent; we are contingent, God is absolute; we are defined, God is the definer; we are held in being by his will, he *is* absolute being.

Verse 6 continues: "You have made heaven, the heaven of heavens, with all their host, the earth and all that is on it, the seas and all that is in them; and you preserve all of them." Therefore, the verse concludes, "the host of heaven worships you." Or, as verse 5 says, his name and glory are "exalted above all blessing and praise."

This is the God (according to v. 7) who chose Abram, changed his name to "father of many peoples" (Abraham), and made a covenant with him to give his offspring the land. What land? Verse 36: "Behold, we are slaves this day; in the land that you gave to our fathers to enjoy."

So there's the issue: Is this great, powerful Creator, Sustainer, and covenant-maker the kind of God who will rescue his people from their sin and his judgment so that this covenant can be fulfilled? Will the story say yes? Or no?

One thing they know for sure: God is righteous. Verse 8 concludes: "You have kept your promise [that is, "You have caused your word to stand"], for *you are righteous.*" Beneath all his other attributes they affirm at the outset of this story, this is beyond question: God is righteous. That is, he does what is right. Always. Unfailingly. And since there is no standard of rightness outside himself, he is the measure of his own righteous action. What is right is right because it is consistent with the infinitely beautiful glory and value of God. Whatever else he will do, God will never betray his worth. He will never deny himself (2 Tim. 2:13). This is his righteousness.

But will that spell mercy for Israel? Or judgment?

Israel's Rebellion and God's Response

The deliverance from Egypt and the wilderness wandering of the people spelled out God's triumph and care (Neh. 9:9–15). He made a name for himself against Pharaoh—that is, his righteousness moved him to uphold his infinite worth by crushing the arrogance of Pharaoh and his armies (v. 10b). He divided the sea (v. 11). He led his people miraculously by day and night (v. 12). He spoke with them at Mount Sinai and gave them right rules, true laws, and good statutes (v. 13). He gave them bread from heaven and water from the rock, and he sent them to the land (v. 15).

So far, so good. But in verses 16–31, we find six expressions of Israel's rebellion and God's response. And if we ask, "Why do the Levites focus over and over on the sin and failures of Israel?" the answer is this: the people need to know what God is like in those situations, because that is precisely the situation they are in now, in Jerusalem with Nehemiah. Look at the last phrase of verse 33: "We have acted wickedly." Not *they*. *We*.

So the reason they are focusing on Israel's failures in the past is that nothing is more important than to learn from this story what God is like in response to such failures.

Pair #1: Verses 16–17

Israel's Rebellion

"They and our fathers acted presumptuously and stiffened their neck and did not obey your commandments" (v. 16).

God's Response

"But you are a God ready to forgive, gracious and merciful, slow to anger and abounding in steadfast love, and did not forsake them" (v. 17b).

Pair #2: Verses 18-25

Israel's Rebellion

"They . . . made for themselves a golden calf and said, 'This is your God who brought you up out of Egypt,' and . . . committed great blasphemies" (v. 18).

God's Response

"You in your great mercies did not forsake them in the wilderness [but sustained them all the way into the Promised Land, and gave them the land in abundance]" (vv. 19–25).

Pair #3: Verses 26-27

Israel's Rebellion

"They were disobedient and rebelled against you and cast your law behind their back and killed your prophets . . . and they committed great blasphemies" (v. 26).

God's Response

"Therefore you gave them into the hand of their enemies, who made them suffer. And in the time of their suffering they cried out to you and you heard them from heaven, and according to your great mercies you gave them saviors who saved them from the hand of their enemies" (v. 27). In other words, according to God's righteousness, judgment came, but it was not the last word; they cried in their deserved judgment, and God had mercy.

Pair #4: Verse 28

Israel's Rebellion

"But after they had rest they did evil again before you" (v. 28a).

God's Response

"And you abandoned them to the hand of their enemies, so that they had dominion over them. Yet when they turned and cried to you, you heard from heaven, and many times you delivered them according to your mercies" (v. 28b). Again the response of God's righteousness was judgment, but again it was not the last word. They cried out, and God had mercy.

Pair #5: Verses 29b–30a

Israel's Rebellion

"They acted presumptuously and did not obey your commandments, but sinned against your rules" (v. 29b).

God's Response

"Many years you bore with them and warned them by your Spirit through your prophets" (v. 30a).

Pair #6: Verses 30b–31

Israel's Rebellion

"Yet they would not give ear" (v. 30b).

God's Response

"Therefore you gave them into the hand of the peoples of the lands. Nevertheless, in your great mercies you did not make an end of them or forsake them, for you are a gracious and merciful God" (vv. 30c–31). For a third time, God's judgment is mentioned, and again it was not the last word, but mercy came.

Now, how do the Israelites respond to this story of sixfold failure followed by sixfold mercy? The answer is that they cry out again for mercy, as they had so many times before, and they renew the covenant to keep the law of God and to take care of the house of God.

Verse 32 brings the new cry for mercy: "Now, therefore, our God, the great, the mighty, and the awesome God, who keeps covenant and steadfast love, *let not all the hardship seem little to you that has come upon us.*" In other words, "Look with pity on us again, as you have so many times, and save us."

The renewal of the covenant comes in verse 38: "Because of all this we make a firm covenant in writing." Chapter 10, then, records the terms of the covenant, which can be summed up as a renewed commitment to keep the law of God—"[We] enter into a curse and an oath to walk in God's Law" (v. 29)—and a renewed commitment to take care of the house of God—"We also take on ourselves the obligation to give yearly a third part of a shekel for the service of the house of our God" (v. 32). This is followed by seven more references to the house of God in the rest of the chapter.

The Lesson for Us

So what is the lesson from this for us in our sin-caused, God-sent distress? Is the lesson that we should look back on all the amazing mercies of God in Israel's history, and then, and in the hope of more mercy, make a new resolution to obey God better?

There are (at least) two major problems with that message. One is this: the odds are not very good, after Israel's history of failure, that it is going to go better. After a thousand years of failure, are the Israelites of Nehemiah's time going to be the generation where the failure stops? The odds are not good, and therefore, the hope is not great.

The other problem is worse. Look at Nehemiah 9:33: "Yet you have been righteous in all that has come upon us." All the hardship, all the distress, all the slavery is just. God has dealt righteously with Israel. He has upheld the worth of his glory. He has done them no wrong. It is right that they are in distress. God's judgments are righteous.

So maybe this time God is saying: "I'm done being your patsy. I will not be mocked by your fickle allegiance to me. I *am* slow to anger. But a thousand years is long enough. I have passed over the trampling of my glory so many times you can't even count them. My mercy is over. My righteousness is vindicated in your judgment."

In other words, the two problems at the end of Nehemiah 9–10—and at the end of the Old Testament—are that (1) God has not yet acted to prevent the disobedience that brings judgment, so it keeps happening; and (2) God has not yet acted to vindicate his righteousness *in* mercy, so that the two are in perfect harmony and we don't have to fear that his mercy will run out because it is against his righteousness.

The reason those two problems exist is that the story that the Levites tell here is not complete. You can't know God fully from a story that is not fully told, and Israel's story is not complete without the Messiah. And these are two of the very problems Messiah Jesus came into the world to solve.

What Jesus Came to Do

Jesus lifted up the cup at the Last Supper and said, "This cup that is poured out for you is the new covenant in my blood" (Luke 22:20). And the promise of the new covenant is: "I will give you a new heart, and a new spirit I will put within you. . . . And I will put my Spirit within you, and cause you to walk in my statutes" (Ezek. 36:26–27). By that blood-bought Spirit, he seals us for the day of redemption (Eph. 1:13; 4:30). He will complete what he has begun, and will perfect us on the day of Christ (Phil. 1:6, 10). Because of the blood of Christ—the blood of the new covenant—we are kept in him. And the day is coming—really and surely coming—when we will sin no more.

That's the remedy for the first problem, the endless cycle of failure-mercy, failure-mercy, failure-mercy. Jesus sealed the new covenant by his blood. The day of failure will soon be over. Till then, we are sealed by the Spirit and are fighting sin by his power.

Not only did the story of Israel in Nehemiah 9 cry out for a day when God himself would conquer our sinful failures, but it also cried out for a resolution of the tension between God's righteousness and his mercy. How could God pass over so many blasphemous failures in Israel and still be righteous? How could he uphold the worth of his own name when, time after time, he passed over the defamation of his name in the God-belittling sins of his people? The Old Testament saints knew in their hearts that the blood of bulls and of goats was not vindication of the worth of God. It was just a pointer.

And what that blood pointed to is Romans 3:25: God put Christ forward "as a propitiation by his blood, to be received by faith. This *was to show God's righteousness*, because in his divine forbearance he had passed over former sins."

He had passed over former sins. Oh, indeed he had. And Nehemiah 9 is one of the clearest witnesses. Failure-mercy, failure-mercy, failure-mercy. How can this be, and God be righteous? How many murderers and adulterers and idolaters can God send to heaven before someone rightly says, "You don't esteem your holiness and your glory very highly"?

The answer to that indictment is the God-planned death of the Son of God. Shedding the blood of the most valuable being in the universe is God's way of saying: "This much I hate your sin, and this much I love my glory. Never think again that my mercy is cheap, or that it ever conflicts with my righteousness. Once and for all, I have vindicated the worth of my name. My righteousness stands forever *in mercy* for everyone who trusts my Son."

God does not exist for the sake of our enjoying biblical stories; biblical stories exist for the sake of our enjoying God. When the Son of God came into the world to complete the story of Israel—when he died, rose again, took his throne, and sent his Spirit—he was making a name for himself. A name that would last two thousand years. A name, a revelation of who he is and what he is like, so that you might know him and trust him and enjoy him, as he comes to you in your distress, even if it is caused by your own sin and sent by God himself. He is coming to you now, in this chapter, through his Word, to help you in mercy and

in righteousness. Welcome him. Trust him. Enjoy him. That is
why the stories exist.

Reflect and Pray

Reflect on each question, and then take a moment to speak or
write the prayers that grow from those reflections.

1. The point of Bible stories, as John Piper points out, is that
   God makes a name for himself. Why is this good news for
   God's distressed people in Nehemiah 9–10? And why is
   this good news for us today? *Because God allows*
   us to know Him + enjoy
2. This sermon highlights for us the burning, building tension *Him*
   of Old Testament history: does God's righteousness mean *for*
   he will show his sinful people mercy or that he will exercise *who*
   his just judgment against them? In what ways have you *He*
   seen or known this tension? How do we see this tension *is*
   resolved at Calvary? *Christs death + resurrection*
   was final.

   We (I) feel it when under conviction. The reality of the cross is relief.

3. Throughout the prayer in Nehemiah 9, the people recall six
   historic glimpses of Israel's rebellion and God's responses
   of mercy. This pattern gives them confidence to appeal to
   God for fresh mercy as they repent of their own rebellion. Consider the confidence we have as sinners redeemed
   through faith in Christ: he appeals to the Father on our
   behalf, and on the basis of his own substitutionary death
   as our sinless Savior. Read Hebrews 4:14–16 and offer a
   prayer of thanksgiving to the Lord for the assurance he
   gives you in Christ.

Think Like an Expositor

What can we learn from John Piper's sermon? First, it pulls us
upward to the greatness of God. It is indeed personal. It's compas-
sionate. It's clear. But first and foremost, it leads us to contemplate
the glorious God who is above all—the Lord God who is exalted
in this portion of his inspired Word and throughout the Scriptures.

Piper has written a book in which he specifically addresses

men ordained as preaching elders or pastors who preach the Word regularly to the gathered congregations of God's people. Although that category of speaking the Word does not apply to us all, we can all learn from the wisdom of *The Supremacy of God in Preaching*. All of us who handle and communicate the Scriptures would do well to heed the substance of this reminder:

> People are starving for the greatness of God. But most of them would not give this diagnosis of their troubled lives. The majesty of God is an unknown cure. There are far more popular prescriptions on the market, but the benefit of any other remedy is brief and shallow. Preaching that does not have the aroma of God's greatness may entertain for a season, but it will not touch the hidden cry of the soul: "Show me thy glory!"[1]

We're often supremely concerned to be practical and attentive to the needs of those who listen and those who come to study. We might fear they'll think such an exalted message is irrelevant in the face of today's pressing needs. Piper speaks to this:

> God himself is the necessary subject matter of our preaching, in his majesty and truth and holiness and righteousness and wisdom and faithfulness and sovereignty and grace. I don't mean we shouldn't preach about nitty-gritty, practical things like parenthood and divorce and AIDS and gluttony and television and sex. What I mean is that every one of those things should be swept up into the holy presence of God and laid bare to the roots of its Godwardness or godlessness.[2]

But how can a person sweep people up in this way? Most people do not have such dramatic sweeping ability, to state the issue mildly. But I am quite certain Piper would protest the question. The same one who claims people should be swept up into the holy presence of God as they hear the Word proclaimed would tell us,

---

[1] John Piper, *The Supremacy of God in Preaching* (Grand Rapids, MI: Baker, 1990), 9.
[2] Ibid., 12.

without a doubt, that the preacher's job is to be a humble, prayerful, diligent expositor of the living and active Word of God, which does the sweeping, by God's Spirit, when that Word is heard.

In fact, this sermon from Nehemiah 9–10 sweeps us up into the holy presence of God by digging down into the structure and content of the text—laying out with care those six patterned passages that, with growing crescendo, tell the repeated story of Israel's rebellion, God's just punishment, their misery and crying out, and God's response of mercy on them. It takes some work to lay it all out and to follow the laying out. But the result is that the pattern of sin and mercy embedded in the story gets burned into our hearts—so that we cry out for mercy, and finally cry out for our Savior, the Lord Jesus Christ.

In the end, it's all about expounding the Word faithfully, in order to let it speak:

> All Christian preaching should be the exposition and application of biblical texts. Our authority as preachers sent by God rises and falls with our manifest allegiance to the text of Scripture. I say "manifest" because there are so many preachers who say they are doing exposition when they do not ground their assertions explicitly—"manifestly"—in the text. They don't show their people clearly that the assertions of their preaching are coming from specific, readable words of Scripture that the people can see for themselves.[3]

In a sermon at Bethlehem Baptist Church on May 12, 2009, Piper stopped to comment on the activity of preaching: "The preacher's job," he said, "is to minimize his own opinions and deliver the truth of God. Every sermon should explain the Bible and then apply it to people's lives." Preaching the Word, he said, is "expository exultation."[4]

---

[3] Ibid., 41.
[4] http://www.desiringgod.org/articles/what-i-mean-by-preaching.

6

Celebrating!
A Moment of Joy
in Jerusalem

Part I: Nehemiah 11:1–12:26

Carrie Sandom

When *Titanic* left Southampton on April 10, 1912, there were more than two thousand people on board. The passenger log brought together an amazing cross section of people. Those traveling in first class included members of the aristocracy, businessmen, politicians, military personnel, industrialists, bankers, and professional sportsmen. Those traveling in second class included doctors, professors, journalists, lawyers, and clergymen. Those in third class included servants, nannies, nursemaids, and immigrants moving to the United States to start a new life.

Lists are important. They are designed to give information in an easily digestible form, and if your name is supposed to be on a particular list, then it's natural to check and make sure. So when it comes to lists of names in the Bible, we should not skip over them or think they are unimportant. The names may be unfamiliar to us, but they belonged to *real* people who were involved in *real* events.

The book of Nehemiah has lots of lists. Chapter 7 records a list of people who returned from the exile. Chapter 10 records the names of all the leaders who signed the binding agreement made after the reading of the Law. In Chapter 11, there is a list of people who volunteered to live in Jerusalem (vv. 1–19), together with a list of those who settled in the surrounding towns and villages (vv. 20–36). Chapter 12 records a list of all the priests and Levites who returned from the exile (12:1–26).

A few years ago, I was in Washington, DC, and visited the Vietnam Veterans Memorial with a friend who had lost her brother in the conflict. Deb had been there many times before, but she wanted to show me where Scott was listed on the wall. There are more than fifty-eight thousand names on the wall. They are not listed alphabetically, as at most other war memorials, but rather chronologically, according to the day people were killed. It would have taken me a long time to locate the right panel, but Deb knew exactly where to find Scott's name. That is what happens when you're connected to someone whose name appears on a list.

The lists recorded in Nehemiah are no different. For generations, people would have pored over them to see where their fathers, grandfathers, and great-grandfathers were mentioned. But these lists were not merely for future generations to look at and take pride in their ancestry; rather, they are an enduring testimony to God's continuing faithfulness to his covenant promises.

Think, for example, of the promises God made to Abraham in Genesis 12—that he would have many descendants who would become a great nation, living in their own land and enjoying God's blessing and rule. Those promises were still being worked out in

Nehemiah's day. Or think of the promises God made to his people in Ezekiel 36—that he would bring the exile to an end and bring them back into their own land, and that he would give them new hearts and his Spirit so they could follow his laws. Those promises were just starting to be fulfilled here.

The lists of names in Nehemiah form an important part of the Bible's demonstration of God's faithfulness to his promises. He had brought his people back from exile; the temple had been restored; the walls of Jerusalem had been rebuilt; and they had recommitted themselves to obeying God's laws. This was a time of rededication and renewal, and, if you had been there, you would have wanted your name to appear on one of these lists.

Chapters 11 and 12 describe for us the practical consequences of the people's renewed commitment. In this first section (11:1–12:26), their renewal is demonstrated by the repopulation of Jerusalem. The city was large and spacious, but few people were living there because the houses had not yet been rebuilt (7:4). If the city was to be properly restored, it needed inhabitants. Jerusalem was a hugely significant place for the covenant community because of the temple—the place where God dwelt among his people; where his Word was read and taught; and where offerings and sacrifices were made every day.

We are told at the start of chapter 11 that the leaders were already living in Jerusalem; those who would join them were decided by the casting of lots, and some volunteered to live there (vv. 1–2). In total, a tenth of the people who had returned from exile were chosen to live in Jerusalem, and it would have been costly for them to do so. The city was large enough, but it was derelict, and the houses needed rebuilding. There was a lot of hard work to be done, but these people were willing to move there. This is what happens when God's Word is at work in his people: they are willing make sacrifices.

In addition to the leaders, some men from the tribes of Judah (vv. 4–6) and Benjamin (vv. 7–9) were living in Jerusalem. These were the tribes that had formed the southern kingdom of Judah after Israel divided into two during the reign of Rehoboam. The kings of Judah had all come from David's line and, broadly speaking, had kept the temple as the focus of the nation's covenant life. God's kindness to his people meant that his promises to David were still intact—there would be a King from the tribe of Judah, born in David's line, who would defeat God's enemies and reign forever. The good news from this little list is that those promises were still standing! ⟍ Jesus !

Also living in Jerusalem at that time were priests who were responsible for the work inside the temple (vv. 10–14). This included the presentation of daily offerings and sacrifices, keeping the Sabbath regulations, performing the ritual purifications, and running the sacred assemblies and annual festivals. There were also Levites who were in charge of the work outside the house of God (vv. 15–18). They included scribes and teachers of the law who led the people in prayers and services of thanksgiving. They were responsible for instructing the people and making God's Word clear to them (see 8:8).

The gatekeepers are also listed (v. 19). They were responsible for guarding the temple gates and making sure people didn't enter the wrong court. The temple was made up of four courts and two inner chambers, and there were strict regulations regarding access into each area. The outer court, the court of the Gentiles, was open to everyone. The next, the court of women, was open only to Israelite men and women; the next was open only to Israelite men; but the fourth, the innermost court, was open only to the priests. Dominated by an enormous bronze altar, it was where the daily offerings and sacrifices were made.

Inside the innermost court were two chambers—the outer chamber was the Holy Place, which contained, among other things, the golden altar of incense; and the inner chamber was the Most Holy Place, which contained the ark of the covenant. Only the high priest was allowed to enter this inner chamber, but only on the annual Day of Atonement. Why was the Most Holy Place so off limits? Because this was where God dwelt by his Spirit. This was the focal point of the temple, and all the other chambers and courts were arranged around it. God was living in the midst of his people, but direct access into his presence was forbidden—except for the high priest on just one day each year. *Until Jesus!*

These, then, were the people who lived in the city of Jerusalem. The rest of chapter 11 lists the residents of the towns of Judah (v. 20), the villages of Judah to the south of Jerusalem (vv. 25–30), and the villages of Benjamin to the north of the city (vv. 31–36). So important was this phase of Israel's history that people's names and the places where they lived were recorded for posterity. But it's clear that the city of Jerusalem and, in particular, the temple were the main focus. It is surely no accident that all the roles mentioned in these lists were connected with the temple—gatekeepers, singers, musicians, scribes, and so forth. This is then further emphasized by the lists of priests and Levites recorded in chapter 12—first of all, during the days of Jeshua, who was most likely the high priest when the temple was being rebuilt (vv. 1–11), and then during the days of Joiakim, who was high priest after him (vv. 12–26).

Well, what are we to make of all these lists today? There are two things to consider.

The People's Joyful Anticipation as God's Promises Are Being Fulfilled

This was a new chapter for the people of God. Exiled for seventy years, they had no place of their own to live and, because the sacrificial system had been suspended, no way of preserving their covenant relationship with God. But now, with the restoration of the temple and the rebuilding of the walls, the people of God had returned to Jerusalem. God's Word was at the heart of their communal life together and the sacrificial system was up and running once again. The faithful God had brought his people back from exile, back into their own land, and back into covenant relation-ship with him—just as he had said he would.

The people of God had listened to the Word of God and had committed themselves to obeying that Word, even though it was costly for them to do so. The fruit of their renewed commitment is seen in their willingness to make costly sacrifices and move into the city of Jerusalem—the city that was springing back to life as the people once again put their trust in their promise-keeping God.

But for those of us who live further down the Bible's timeline, who live on the other side of the cross and have even more evidence of God's faithfulness to his promises, doesn't this mean that our joy and our anticipation (and our willingness to make costly sacrifices) should be even greater than theirs? We have seen their joyful anticipation as God's promises are being fulfilled, but this should lead to . . .

Our Joyful Realization That God's Promises Have Been Fulfilled in the Lord Jesus Christ

At Nehemiah's point in salvation history, everything was geared around the temple, the place of God-ordained worship and God-ordained sacrifice. The people of God were enjoying the benefits of their covenant relationship with God, but they did not have direct access into his presence. The temple was the means by which sinful people could be brought back into relationship with a holy God, but direct access into his presence was not possible because of their sin. The entrance to the Most Holy Place had an enormous curtain in front of it; the restoration of the temple meant they once again could come near to God—but not that near!

How much more, therefore, should we rejoice at God's faithfulness because his promises have been fulfilled in the Lord Jesus Christ. He is the Mediator of the new covenant; he is our Great High Priest, who intercedes with God on our behalf; and his blood is the one true sacrifice for sin.

In the book of Hebrews, we read that it is impossible for the blood of bulls and goats to take away sins (10:4). But when Jesus died, he took the punishment that should have been ours. He propitiated God's wrath and dealt with our sins once and for all. This means that "we have been made holy through the sacrifice of the body of Jesus Christ once for all" (v. 10 NIV). The temple curtain has been torn and he has opened the way for us to enjoy direct access into God's presence.

God's promises of a return from exile were only partially fulfilled in Nehemiah's generation, but Jesus's death has opened the way into God's presence. So, "Since we have confidence to enter the Most Holy Place by the blood of Jesus, by a new and living way opened for us through the curtain, that is, his body, and since we have a great high priest over the house of God, let us draw near to God with a sincere heart and with the full assurance that faith brings" (Heb. 10:19–22a NIV).

A few years ago, an American family moved from Washington, DC, to central London and joined the church where I was working. Mike had worked at the White House during the George W. Bush administration, and he reckoned there were seventeen different security checks he had to go through before he got anywhere near the Oval Office. He worked for the president, but he couldn't just waltz into his office. He didn't have that kind of access.

But do you remember those iconic photos of President John F. Kennedy at his desk in the Oval Office with his two-year-old son playing at his feet? John Jr. didn't have to go through seventeen security checks; he had direct access to his father's presence. And so it is with Christ. He has direct access to his Father's presence in the throne room of heaven, and by his blood, he has opened direct access for us all.

God's people who returned from exile in Babylon shared a moment of joy in Jerusalem, although it was only fleeting. How much more, therefore, should we rejoice and give thanks because we now have the permanent solution to the problem of sin and

Jesus has opened direct access into God's presence. They shared a moment of joy with each other in Jerusalem. We look forward to an eternity of joy with all God's people in the New Jerusalem.

After *Titanic* sank on April 15, 1912, there was only one list of names that carried any significance: the list of known survivors. It did not matter what lists their names had appeared on at the beginning of the voyage; after the sinking, the only one that really mattered was the list of those who were still alive.

The same is true for us. Whatever lists your name may have appeared on in the past—your Sunday school attendance list, your high school graduation list, your college roll of honor—the only one that really matters is the list of inhabitants of the New Jerusalem. The Lord Jesus has made it possible for our names to be included on that list, and when we gather around his throne, when the books are opened and that list is read out loud for all to hear—boy, will you listen out for your name!

But here in Nehemiah, the people had recommitted themselves to the covenant that assured this salvation. The repopulation of Jerusalem was the first practical consequence of that renewed commitment. Their willingness to move into the derelict city and rebuild it, and their renewed confidence that God would be faithful to his promises, were very evident. God had started something new, and they eagerly anticipated the fulfillment of all his promises.

Think Like an Expositor (Part I)

Carrie Sandom, Jenny Salt, and I (Kathleen Nielson) collaborated on this section of Nehemiah, dividing it into three parts and discussing it as we worked. Looking back over the process, we all mentioned the pleasure and the benefit of working together a bit and hearing each other's feedback. Many teachers work largely or only alone in their preparation; it is always helpful (sometimes confirming, sometimes challenging!) to ask a pastor or a fellow Bible student or teacher for feedback on our notes and thoughts.

Perhaps we might at times seek out a workshop or group where more formal feedback takes place.

Carrie outlined a great process of working through a text—a helpful basic model that anyone can put into practice:

> Preparing for this talk was quite a challenge, as I had not done much exegesis on lists in the Bible before! But I take it that "all Scripture is God-breathed and is useful for teaching, rebuking, correcting and training in righteousness" (2 Tim. 3:16), so God wants us to learn about him from these lists and to live in light of what we learn. The Bible is essentially his revelation of himself to us, so there are always things to learn about God in every passage. The danger with any Old Testament narrative is that we make it about us before properly understanding what it meant for the original readers, so I was concerned not to apply this passage to us in the twenty-first century too soon.
>
> I followed a four-stage process:
>
> 1. Working on the text, with the aim of producing a theme sentence (What does the passage teach?) and an aim for my talk (How should the passage be applied?).
>
> 2. Structuring the talk, with the aim of breaking down the passage into logical sections, producing clear points and headings for each one that overall helped to communicate the theme sentence. Each point needed to be clearly stated, located from the text, and then explained.
>
> 3. Putting the meat on the bones. This is when I thought of illustrations that would serve to bring greater clarity to the points I was making and then worked on the application of the talk (Would I apply each point or make all my points before applying?). Having decided what the conclusion was going to be (and how I would end the talk), I then sketched out the introduction, which needed to provide an arresting start and raise issues that I could return to at the end of the talk (serving the overall aim).
>
> 4. Writing the talk. Having decided on a theme sentence and aim for the talk, I finalized the structure with headings and

points, solidified some illustrations, the application, the conclusion, and the introduction, then wrote the verbatim script
from scratch.

Carrie added some really helpful comments about just how she
worked on the text:

The first thing to consider was context—the historical context
(Where are God's people in the story of the Bible?), the theological context (What's happened to the promises God made
to Abraham, Moses, and David?), and the literary context
(Where are we in the narrative of Nehemiah?).

The next thing was to analyze the text. What do we learn
about God here? What repeated themes/phrases are there?
What is the significance of the geographical references? What
is the significance of the names/roles? What would we lose if
this passage *wasn't* here? What comes immediately after this
passage?

The next thing was to consider what this passage meant
for the original readers. What would they have learned about
God? Why was this such an exciting time for Israel?

Finally, I had to consider what this passage means for us.
How are things different for us? How are they the same? For
example, Jerusalem is no longer the focus of our covenant
life together and the temple is no longer a focus of our worship. The risen and ascended Lord Jesus is our temple and the
one who makes access to God possible. Therefore, how much
more reason do we have for praise, thanksgiving, and anticipation of the life to come in the New Jerusalem?

———

Part II: Nehemiah 12:27–43

Jenny Salt

One word sums up this section well: *joy*! In fact, the celebration in these verses might be seen as the climax of the joy that builds throughout the second half of the book of Nehemiah, as the people were spiritually revived around God's Word and then lived out the effects of that revival together.

We've seen that there was joyful anticipation of a new start in the holy city, the Word of God was once again at the center of the community, the temple with its sacrificial system was up and running, and the city had new inhabitants.

Now, in 12:27–43, the people of God prepared to dedicate the wall of Jerusalem with great joy because of God's faithfulness. There was no sense of "We'd *better* be joyful" or "We *should* be joyful." They were not being *told* to be joyful. They *were* joyful.

To tell these people to be joyful as they were about to dedicate the wall would have been a bit like a friend saying, "C'mon, rejoice!" to a beautiful bride on her wedding day; like a midwife telling a first-time dad with his newborn baby safely in his arms, "Now, I want you to be joyful about your new baby!"; or like a mother telling her child to be joyful as she puts a big bowl of ice cream in front of him when he was expecting fruit for dessert!

These are ridiculous scenarios because in each case, joy is a natural response. Likewise, there was no need to urge the people of Jerusalem to be joyful. There was no need to say, "Rejoice!" They already were rejoicing.

That's the sense of this part of Nehemiah, as the people dedicated the wall of Jerusalem to the Lord. And yet, as Christians, perhaps sometimes we find it hard to relate to that kind of joy. We might think, "I know God wants me to be joyful, I know I should be joyful, but I don't always feel joyful." Is it a matter of gritting our teeth and just doing it; just being joyful?

How *is* joy fostered among God's people? Keep that question in mind as we work through this part of Nehemiah.

Observing the Joy in This Passage

If we go all the way to the end of this section, to verse 43, we read that the people of God rejoiced with great joy, and their joy was heard far away. What had brought them to this place of great joy? It had been quite a journey.

All the way back in chapter 1, Nehemiah heard the news that those who had returned to Jerusalem and Judah were in great trouble and shame, and the wall of Jerusalem was broken down and its gates destroyed. To set things right, he faced hardship and opposition from surrounding peoples, and problems from within the community. It was a long, hard slog—with lots of setbacks, opposition, and disappointments. But now, finally, everything was coming together. The wall had been built, the city repopulated, the Word of God read and explained, and God restored to the center of their community. The day of dedication had arrived. How were they going to prepare for this day?

First, in verse 27, the Levites were brought into the city. Apart from those who had moved and now lived in Jerusalem, the community of God's people lived in the surrounding towns. This included the Levites. But on this special day, it was all hands on deck!

And it wasn't just the Levites. In verses 27–29, we read that the Levites, the singers, and the musicians all came together to lead the people in worship and to celebrate with gladness, thanksgiving, singing, and cymbals, harps, and lyres.

Here was the community preparing to celebrate. What did that involve? Verse 30 tells us that the priests and Levites purified themselves, and they also purified the people, the gates, and the wall. Here, perhaps, we get a picture of a big "spring clean"— getting everything spic and span, shiny and clean for the big day. But this purification was more about preparing to come into the presence of God, the One who is holy.

It's not clear what the purifying of the priests and Levites actually involved. We know from other Scripture passages that it might have included ritual washing of themselves and their clothes; it might have included fasting and abstaining from sex; and it might have involved sacrifices. Perhaps it was similar to the way God's people purified themselves when Moses instructed the people to prepare to meet God at Mount Sinai (Exodus 19). Whatever the purification involved, the point was to prepare everything and everyone in the holy city to come into the presence of the Lord.

Then we read of two choirs that formed a procession on the wall itself (Neh. 12:31–39). What would that have looked like? Have you ever seen a large choir, all garbed up, all highly organized, all in position, singing their hearts out in beautiful harmony? Or picture a marching band, moving as one, playing and marching with great pride and practiced choreography. Well, bring those two images together and then add some—and that helps us to imagine what this procession would have looked like!

One of the two choirs was accompanied by Ezra the scribe, and in verses 31–37, we read how they proceeded south on the wall to the Dung Gate (probably starting from the Valley Gate) and ended up at the Water Gate. (It might be helpful to have a map of Jerusalem in front of you so you can see where the various gates were positioned.) The other choir was accompanied by Nehemiah, and this procession headed the opposite way, going north on the wall and stopping at the Gate of the Guard (vv. 38–39).

In other words, this great procession was marching and singing right on top of the wall that had been rebuilt, nearly encircling the city. What a spectacle! What a sight to inspire celebration for all the people!

For those who had eyes to see and hearts that marveled, the sight and the mention of these gates and walls, the Dung Gate or Fountain Gate, the Fish Gate or Water Gate, or any of the other gates and parts of the wall, would have brought back fresh memories of their recent work of rebuilding. It had been an amazing community event, not without danger, but with a leader, Nehemiah, who knew the good hand of God was upon their work, a leader who prayed and acted in faith to do God's will.

Watching this procession would have been like smelling a certain fragrance that takes us back to a childhood memory; like hearing a certain song that reminds us of a person; or like looking at some photos that bring back memories and emotions associated with a special place. For the people of God in the holy city, seeing the procession of Levites, priests, singers, and leaders on the wall that so recently had been broken down but now was built, by their very own hands, would have filled their hearts with joy.

Why? Because they were looking at nothing less than evidence of God's amazing faithfulness.

Not so long ago, Nehemiah had inspected the broken-down wall at night. Not so long ago, Sanballat and Tobiah had said the wall wouldn't be able to hold a fox (Neh. 4:2–3)! Not so long ago, there had been mocking, laughing, and outright threats. But now, look—there was a procession on the wall, and the people of God were coming together to give thanks to the Lord. To see and acknowledge his faithful hand in their unfolding story gave them great joy.

There is nothing casual or random in this account of the procession. For example, the references to David are not incidental. David is mentioned in relation to musical instruments (v. 36), as well as to parts of the wall, such as the stairs of the city of David above the house of David (v. 37). The mentioning of David in this account evokes memories of God's faithfulness to promises made to his anointed king.

Similarly, even if we tend to skim over them in our reading, the lists of names in these verses—names of men like Zechariah (v. 35), who could trace his ancestry all the way back to Asaph, one of the leaders of worship in the time of King David—had immense significance for the people of God. These names were significant because they reminded the people (and us) of a continuity of leadership, a continuity that we see in all of God's Word. They take us back to the promises made to Abraham, which pointed forward to Abraham's seed—that is, Jesus Christ.

The sight of this procession, as God's people remembered the continuity of his promises to them, would have made their hearts swell with joy. They were seeing his amazing faithfulness.

What were the choirs singing? Perhaps they were singing Psalm 48:

> Walk about Zion, go around her,
>   number her towers,
> consider well her ramparts,
>   go through her citadels,
> that you may tell the next generation
>   that this is God,
> our God forever and ever.
>   He will guide us forever. (vv. 12–14)

That psalm from David's day offered fitting words for this day—a day of celebrating God's continued faithfulness. And this is our God today, our God forever and ever.

The procession finished in the temple: "So both choirs of those who gave thanks stood in the house of God" (Neh. 12:40a). The people were gathered there. The priests offered great sacrifices, and all the people celebrated with great joy.

There is something wonderfully climactic about these verses. Everything had been leading up to this moment: God's work in raising up godly leaders such as Zerubbabel, Jeshua, Ezra, and Nehemiah, and his work of reestablishing the temple worship and renewing his covenant through the practice of sacrifices and the preaching of his Word.

So now the people rejoiced in all that the Lord had done: "And they offered great sacrifices that day and rejoiced, for God had made them rejoice with great joy; the women and children also rejoiced. And the joy of Jerusalem was heard far away" (v. 43). The word translated as "rejoice" in various forms is repeated five times in this verse. Joy was expressed in praise, thanksgiving, sacrifices, singing, and music. Joy was expressed by everyone: leaders, singers, priests, Levites, men, women, and children. Everyone was involved as they celebrated with great joy. This was a high point in the history of God's people.

Oh, yes, there had been other times of great celebration—for example, in Ezra 3, which recounts the laying of the temple foundation. At the gathering to dedicate that foundation, there had been great joy, but also great weeping—because the temple was not nearly as impressive as it had been before the exile. The sound was heard far away, but that joy was mixed with sadness. Again, there had been great joy at the dedication of the rebuilt temple when it was completed (Ezra 6:16). And more recently, after the rebuilt wall had been completed, at the worship ceremony where the Law was read and explained to the people, there had been another time of rejoicing "because they had understood the words that were declared to them" (Neh. 8:12).

But this occasion was especially joyful, with no mix of sadness in the joy of Jerusalem that could be heard far away. It might have been like hearing from afar the roar of a crowd at a sporting event celebrating the victory of their team. What a day! If you had to sum up these verses in one word, it would be *joy*!

Learning from the Joy in This Passage

So what do we learn about joy in these verses? How is joy fostered in God's people?

First, we learn that *joy is God-centered*. The joy in this scene came to the people as a result of being in the very presence of God, gathered in the temple as his purified people, together giving thanks to him. Notice what verse 43 says: "God had made them rejoice with great joy." Not only did their joy come from being in God's presence, but it came from him. He was the living and active source of his people's joy as they worshiped him.

It's the same for us. Joy is fostered in us as we come together as God's people, with God at the center. But it's no longer about meeting in a place, but rather through a person: Jesus Christ, our Savior, who purified us once and for all through his blood. Joy is fostered in our knowing the very presence of God in the Lord Jesus and celebrating that together. It comes in our gathering week by week to worship the Lord as the people of God. Joy comes as we gather at events like The Gospel Coalition's women's conferences, as sisters in Christ, worshiping God together.

Indeed, the joy of God's people is God-centered.

Second, we learn from this passage, even more specifically, that *joy comes in remembering God's faithfulness*. As the choirs and leaders proceeded around the wall, all who were there would have remembered how the Lord had protected them and enabled them to finish the work. Not so long before, this wall had been broken down, the city empty, and the Word of God neither heard nor understood. Now look! Remembering his faithfulness fosters joy.

It's the same for us, as we together remember our God, who has given us his Son, Jesus Christ, our Great High Priest, who has provided a new and living way through his own blood (Heb. 10:19–20), who has given us the Holy Spirit as "the guarantee of our inheritance" (Eph. 1:14), and who has given us his Word to live by.

But we are so apt to forget as we get caught up in the "stuff" of life. How are we to remember God's faithfulness? We remember by daily preaching the gospel to ourselves, that is, reminding ourselves of the truths of the gospel. We remember by daily saturating our hearts and minds in God's Word, so that God's ways become our "default" ways of thinking and living. We remember by talking with each other, reminding each other of his works day by day. Indeed, the joy of God's people comes in remembering his faithfulness.

Finally, we learn from this passage, most specifically, that *joy comes with thankfulness.* The focus on God and the remembrance of God happened in a certain way: with hearts of thankfulness to God. God's people were celebrating the dedication of the wall "with thanksgiving" (Neh. 12:27). As they remembered what God had done, they responded: they lifted up their hearts and offered him thanksgiving. The choirs are described as companies "that gave thanks" (v. 31)—one word in Hebrew. In other words, one "thanksgiving" went to the north and the other "thanksgiving" went to the south. The choirs were the very embodiment of what they sang: thanksgiving. Thankfulness fosters joy.

If the people of God in Jerusalem were consumed by thankfulness, how much more ought that be true for us who live on this side of the cross? How much more ought that be true for us who know God's faithfulness in the Lord Jesus Christ? Indeed, the joy of God's people comes with thankfulness.

I have some friends who are great examples of joy. They had been serving the Lord in Southeast Asia, but had to return to Australia for a number of reasons, including health issues. In one of their prayer letters while home, here is what they wrote about thankfulness and joy (names and some details have been changed to protect their privacy):

After reading a really fantastic book called *One Thousand Gifts* we have been inspired to keep a family thanksgiving journal, and it has truly brought great joy to think of all the ways we have been blessed, both big and small. We are up to 361 gifts we are thankful for at the moment and are aiming for 1000. When we reach 1000 we are going to celebrate!

Here are some things that have featured in our thanksgiving journal:

- Daddy feeling well enough to take James to school
- falling asleep when it is raining
- fresh lettuce growing in our garden
- a nice cup of Earl Grey tea in the morning
- cuddles from Charlie
- friends bringing gifts of eggs from their own chickens
- Charlie's laugh
- Emily's fat rolls on her thighs

By the way, Emily is a baby; there comes a time when we cease to thank God for those rolls!

These friends have faced some difficult circumstances, but this is a family that is joyful, with a thankfulness that fosters joy. Their thankfulness is centered first of all in the Lord Jesus, and it affects every corner of their lives.

You don't have to tell a bride on her wedding day, you don't have to tell a new parent who looks at a newborn baby, and you don't have to tell a child with a big bowl of ice cream to rejoice.

And you didn't have to tell the people of God in Jerusalem to rejoice with great joy. They just did, because God had made them rejoice: they were God's people, gathered together in his presence with a joy that was God-centered, full of remembering God's faithful works, and overflowing with thanksgiving offered back to him. How much more for us?

And they offered great sacrifices that day and rejoiced, for God had made them rejoice with great joy; the women and children also rejoiced. And the joy of Jerusalem was heard far away. (Neh. 12:43)

Think Like an Expositor (Part II)

If we haven't yet grasped the importance of beginning by reading and observing a text, Jenny Salt reminds us. But notice that she mentions first the crucial and wonderful step of prayer—which somehow we sometimes can rush right through in our process of preparation:

> My approach in preparation was the same approach I use for preparation in any Bible passage:
>
> 1. Pray that the Lord will enable me to understand and prepare faithfully, that I would be seeking the Spirit's help at every point. In the words of Dale Ralph Davis, we need to look "to the God who breathed out this Scripture to give us an understanding of the Scripture."[1]
>
> 2. Print the passage out and read, underline, read, ask questions of the text, read, translate from the original, read, and start to get a "feel" for the passage. I want to get to the point of being able to sum up in one sentence the content and intent of the passage (the "big idea" of the text). This must be the starting point of any teaching from God's Word. If I, as the one teaching from the passage, have not grasped the burden of the text, then it will be much more difficult to be clear and faithful in the teaching.
>
> 3. Because it is set in the OT/post-exilic period, I also want to understand how this passage fits with the overall flow of Scripture. That is, I need to ask, "How do we understand this passage in the light of the cross of Christ?" It's only after asking this question that we can apply the passage to those who live on this side of the cross (that is, us!).

Asked about challenges, Jenny mentioned the difficult process

---

[1] Dale Ralph Davis, *The Word Became Fresh* (Ross-shire, Scotland: Christian Focus, 2006), 2.

of finding the best application for this Old Testament narrative for the lives of the women who would listen, "packaging the talk in such a way that I didn't lose the weight of God's Word but at the same time, communicating it clearly and faithfully to the visible and invisible audience (i.e. the women listening online). It's important to 'know your audience' (as much as possible) whenever you prepare a passage, and so I am always mindful of the responsibility of applying the passage faithfully and helpfully even when I don't know most of the women I am speaking to. (And keeping to time is always a challenge for me!)"

In the end, Jenny stresses both the beauty and the importance of Old Testament narrative as part of our regular diet of Bible study:

> I love the Old Testament and I love "getting my hands dirty" in the preparation—delving into the passage, digging deep, and gaining a better understanding of God's Word. I am always struck by the fact that God does not change, and so as we study the Old Testament, we learn about the God of the whole Bible—his promises, purposes, and how they find their fulfillment in Christ.
>
> But that is also the challenge: to explain the passage in its own right (not use it as a mere springboard for a New Testament theme/passage) and also faithfully to apply the truths of the OT to those who live on this side of the cross (not just tacking the cross onto the end of the Bible talk).

_____

Part III: Nehemiah 12:44-47

Kathleen Nielson

In Nehemiah 11–12, we are seeing what happens when God works in his people through his Word. We're finding the fruit of that dramatic repentance and revival we saw in chapters 8–10, as God's people gathered around his Word. What kinds of fruit have we seen in these chapters so far?

First, Carrie Sandom showed us a people *ready to move* (11:1–12:26)—ready to move in and repopulate Jerusalem, full of anticipation for God's work in that broken-down city. When God works in a people through his Word, first, we've seen they're ready to move! *ready to obey!*

Second, Jenny Salt showed us a people *ready to rejoice* (12:27–43). The repopulated city of Jerusalem began to ring with joyful worship that echoed far! When God works in a people through his Word (even as we experience at a Gospel Coalition conference—or, more important, week by week in church), it brings the kind of joy we spend a lot of our lives longing for. *ready to worship*

And now, finally, because they're so full of joyful worship, we see a people *ready to order their lives to keep it going*. When God works in a people through his Word, *obedience + worship* they're ready to move, and so they're ready for joyful worship—and then they're so full of that joyful worship that they're ready to order their lives to keep it going! *plan obedience*

organized
deliberate

Does that sound a little anticlimactic after such a grand celebration? The joyful songs are still echoing when verse 44 breaks in with, "On that day," and on that day they do *what*? What's the marvelous end to this marvelous passage? They get organized. They put structures and disciplines in place. That does sound a little anticlimactic. This section is like a postscript to the climactic worship scene we've just relished. But it's actually beautiful—surprisingly beautiful.

Here's the thing: we don't live our daily lives in a grand climax of celebration, do we? We *will* someday, when there's no night, only the light of the Lamb, and the New Jerusalem shining like brilliant gems—oh, don't you long for that day! But now we're still on the way to that day, and every grand celebration of our lives brings us back home to an ordinary day of continuing to walk faithfully. But we walk with God's Word to light the way, to show us how to order our lives to keep worship going, day by day, until that day. Martin Luther is known to have said there were only two days on his calendar: this day and *that day*!

Let's make three observations from this final section of Nehemiah 12 (vv. 44–47) about just *how* these people are ordering their lives. Because of the nature of this narrative, we won't be moving consecutively through these verses; rather, we will be digging out three important themes that wind their way through this section that recounts the ordering of worship practices at the center of the people's lives.

Ordering—according to God's Word

First and foremost, God's people are ordering their lives together according to God's Word. They're not making this up as they go; rather, they're instituting worship practices that verse 44 tells us are "required by the Law"—that is, practices that were set forth by Moses in the Pentateuch as God's prescribed rituals of worship. The Law is full of instruction about bringing "the best of the first-fruits" of the land into the house of the Lord: in Deuteronomy 26,

Moses gives a beautiful review of how the people should gather their harvest firstfruits in a basket and carry it to the priest, who would take the basket and set it before the altar of the Lord—all the while rehearsing God's faithfulness in bringing them out of slavery and into such a rich land. In Nehemiah 10, we saw the people covenanting to bring these offerings—and here they are getting them organized.

These regular offerings and contributions, along with tithes every third year for the needy, were to be kept in various store-rooms and carefully apportioned to the priests and Levites—who would then be supported and enabled to devote themselves to their worship duties. In verse 45, we glimpse the priests and Levites at work, performing "the service of their God and the service of purification." We glimpsed these purification rituals in verse 30 of this chapter—and, of course, *many* such rituals were required, to purify the people from all sorts of uncleanness, over and over and over. Sacrifices were to be regularly offered as well—the temple was to be a constantly active center of life and focus for God's people. The singers and gatekeepers crowd into the busy scene also, in verse 45, following the practices begun in the time of David and Solomon, when the temple was first planned and built. In the end, this passage shows *everybody* to be involved, with "all Israel" (v. 47) giving the daily portions and offerings, which are divided up and allotted according to the practices prescribed in the Law. It's quite a system, isn't it?

This temple-centered worship is a huge enterprise, and God obviously cares about every detail of it. The Old Testament is full of the ways God provided for his people to come into his presence and worship him. The people here are honoring God by taking care to order the practices he prescribed. Think about the grand dedication ceremony we just read about: according to verse 47, that represented a gigantic reorganizing effort begun under Zerubbabel, who led the first group of freed exiles back to Jerusalem about a hundred years before this, and who paved the way by rebuilding the temple and reinstituting these temple practices. Now Nehemiah is carrying it on, cementing these practices, all of it as "required by the Law." Nehemiah, we've seen, is a man of the Word—and here, under his leadership, all the momentum of that grand worship is gathered up and carried on in these practices, ordered according to God's Word.

This first observation—that God's people order their lives together according to his Word—speaks right into our lives. For one thing, it reminds us of the basic fact that we are instructed as God's people to order ourselves: the apostle Paul talks about things in the church being done "decently and in order" (1 Cor. 14:40). Paul spends a lot of time in the Epistles explaining how God's people, now called the church, are to be ordered so that robust worship of the Lord Jesus can grow and spread.

The structured organization of the church is not always a welcome idea these days. Have you sensed or felt this anti-institutional mentality that's tired of formal, organized structures and just longs for good personal interaction? Kevin DeYoung and Ted Kluck wrote a great book about this, with a wonderfully "in-your-face" title: *Why We Love the Church: In Praise of Institutions and Organized Religion.*[2] In that book, they respond biblically to this cultural "dissing" of, as they say, "the organizational, institutional, hierarchical, programmatic, weekly services view of church."[3] A lot of people would rather just read their Bibles with a friend over coffee, just get a group together on the spot and see how the Spirit leads, or just listen online to a good sermon—or read a good blog and then post a few comments.

In fact, we probably need to do more reading the Bible with people over coffee, more meeting with groups to talk and pray—and enjoying a great blog is great! But the point here is that what confronts us in Scripture from beginning to end is God's call to his

---

[2] Kevin DeYoung and Ted Kluck, *Why We Love the Church: In Praise of Institutions and Organized Religion* (Chicago: Moody, 2009).
[3] Ibid, 18.

people to order their lives around regular worship practices, regular gathering together, with carefully appointed and qualified leaders, faithful financial contributions and accounting of that giving, organized care for the needy, often musical praise and worship, and always front and center, the reading and teaching of God's Word. Through these kinds of structures, the joyful enthusiasm of God's people can be not only carried on but also *passed* on to others and to the next generations. Without these kinds of structures, passing on that joyful enthusiasm often just doesn't happen.

Many of us probably know the temptation to let our busyness pull us away from regular connection with the structure of church life, with its disciplines of meeting together and serving one another, with active respect for leadership. All of this takes a huge commitment, as we order our lives around these God-ordained means by which God blesses and grows his people. Some of us might struggle to connect not so much *with* the church but *within* the church—that is, to find the most fruitful places as women to serve within the structure of leadership that we want to support with lives of faith, love, and holiness with self-control (1 Tim. 2:15). This can be challenging. But what motivates and empowers us today to meet this challenge of connecting ourselves well within the order of God's people? Here's the beautiful advantage we have: we are not fitting ourselves into a system of temple regulations that point toward a promise, as we've seen in Nehemiah. We believers on this side of the cross are part of a living thing, a body, Christ's body—a living temple of his presence. So this may be challenging, but this is our *life*, as the Word explains it to us.

So let's keep on actively loving the church. Let's keep on loving the church because we love the *Head* of the church, Christ, who gave himself up for us and who makes us pure and beautiful (Eph. 5:27). Here's the ultimate ordering of God's people presented in God's Word: God gave his own Son as "head over all things to the church" (Eph. 1:22). For love of our Head, we believers order ourselves as his people according to his Word.

My husband and I both grew up in families who loved the church and who were involved in church families' lives. We've tried to analyze what kept us from getting "burnt out," as they say, or cynical. We've concluded that our families simply really did love the church and delighted in God's people, because at heart, they loved the Lord of the church—and it was catching!

This is one of the joys of serving with The Gospel Coalition, a ministry that doesn't compete with the church but aims to serve the church by serving its leaders and members. And that's one of the joys of the TGC women's conferences: that women who come from churches all over the world might be encouraged and a bit more equipped to go back and love and serve those churches (or to find one, if they haven't yet)—living out this pattern we glimpse in Nehemiah 12 of God's people with lives filled with worship ordered according to his Word.

Ordering—in Dependence on His Promises

The second observation follows logically: God's people are ordering their lives in dependence on his promises. This part of the book has King David on its mind, doesn't it? "David the man of God" was mentioned back in verse 24, and also in verses 36 and 37. And we've seen here in verse 45 that the singers and gatekeepers follow what David and Solomon set up. Then in verse 46, we return to David's history: "For long ago in the days of David and Asaph [one of the psalmists who served under King David as a music director] there were directors of the singers, and there were songs of praise and thanksgiving to God." Why all these mentions of David?

Well, just as the people have been recording all these names, faithfully tracing the promised seed of Abraham, so here, as they keep tracing the links to King David, they're not just holding on to traditions; they're actually putting themselves in the stream of God's promises. David was a key figure in the unfolding of God's promises, and these people know that. They were especially reminded of that as they collected and sang the psalms during the period of rebuilding, for the psalms are full of promises to David. Psalm 89, for example, celebrates these promises directly:

> You have said, "I have made a covenant with my chosen
>   one;
>   I have sworn to David my servant:
> 'I will establish your offspring forever,
>   and build your throne for all generations.'" (vv. 3–4)

As the people sing the songs of David and follow the worship practices commanded by David—and highlight the fact that they're doing so—they are setting themselves in a stream of promise, a covenant stream. The stream doesn't *look* so promising at this point: they don't even have their own king anymore. But they are setting the temple service back in motion, following God's Word, keeping King David in their sights—they are, in effect, putting their faith in God's promises, even when the fulfillment is invisible. They'll sing loudly those words from Psalm 2 about God, who sets his king on Zion, his holy hill. And a faithful remnant will keep singing until the promised king appears.

This second observation also speaks right into our lives right now, challenging us to ask what we're depending on as we order ourselves in the church. What's our worship all about? Is it all about our own experience right now, or do we get how we fit into a larger story? Do we grasp that we as God's people are recipients of a long stream of promises, a covenant stream that flows right to Jesus? The book of Nehemiah helps us here, as we see the people continually looking back over their history. We begin to see that this is our history, too, and that we in the church today are incredibly privileged to live in the part of the story where the promises have been fulfilled and are now flowing fast to the end.

We get to sing about the promised King Jesus, the Son of David who *came*—and we sing, too, about his coming again. We have the final and full orchestral version of "songs of praise and thanksgiving to God" (Neh. 12:46). Let's not forget why we sing. As God's people, we sing not just for the satisfaction of our own emotional expression; we sing ultimately to declare and celebrate God's glorious promises, all fulfilled in his glorious Son. We in the church today are in a long line of faithful singers. It's a line that stretches ahead to the climax, when the music will burst from all the corners of heaven and earth and under the earth. What a wonder to be part of it. What a joy.

Ordering—with Joy

And here we are at the third observation: joy, again! These people are ordering their lives: (1) according to the Word of God; (2) in dependence on the promises of God; and (3) with joy. This final section of Nehemiah 12 is all about their ordering of their lives, yes, but it certainly doesn't come across as just a matter of legalistic rules. Did you notice the words at the end of verse 44, right after all the laborious categories of offerings and workers: "For Judah *rejoiced* over the priests and the Levites who ministered"? Of course this joy doesn't jump out and surprise us here in the text; the word *joy* has been woven into the whole book—especially vividly in that amazing Bible study scene of chapter 8, and then climactically in the joyful worship whose echoes haven't yet died away as we read these verses. That joy just leaps naturally into this next section—and all this order according to the Law actually becomes a source of continuing joy.

Think of how the people might have chafed under these laws at this point. They were poor, and they really needed to get their farms and houses in order: what a drain, to spend so much time and effort on all these temple goings-on, all these complicated offerings and tithes. Or think of the temple workers themselves. Don't you wonder whether they were tempted to complain about God's ordering of *them*? Only one tribe, Levi, was designated by God to work in the temple, and only one branch of that tribe could be priests: the descendants of Aaron, Moses's brother, the first high priest. How was that fair? I'd bet that some of the non-Levites wished they could do what the Levites were called to do. And I'd bet that some of the Levites who weren't in Aaron's line wished *they* could be priests—and probably some of them would have made better priests than some of the sons of Aaron. All this ordering; we can chafe at it, can't we?

Or we can rejoice in it. That's the other option. It's a much better option, because it opens up the blessing of joy that comes in following God's order according to his Word. God's order is beautiful because he's God. He's the God who made order from the beginning, when he took that formless void and said, "Let there be light," and then separated the light from the darkness, and called the light day and the darkness night, and set the sun to rule the day and the moon to rule the night, and on and on in a whole progression of order that, when we embrace it, gives us the greatest joy. God's order is beautiful because he is God.

This picture of God's people worshiping according to his order and so finding joy is hugely instructive for us. It's easy to chafe against God's order in all kinds of ways—that's our natural bent. But it's not the direction of joy. The direction of joy is to look deeply into God's Word, to put our faith in the promises of that Word, and then to rejoice as God's people in obeying that Word.

Of course, this joy isn't just for us—ultimately, it brings glory to God, who receives the praise of our joyful songs. *And* this joy draws others: remember, the joy rings out of Jerusalem and is heard far away (v. 43)! This joy is meant to rise up and to spread out—ultimately from Jerusalem into all Judea and Samaria, and to the ends of the earth (Acts 1:8).

We Are Not Finished

There's one more thing to say. You know what it is. In Nehemiah 11–12, we've seen that when God works in his people through his Word, they're ready to move; they're ready to rejoice together in worship; and they're ready to order their lives to keep that worship going. What else do we need to say? We need to say that these people couldn't do it. They saw it and aimed for it—and there was this one brief, shining moment of joy in Jerusalem that lets us glimpse it—like a lot of other shining moments in the Old Testament that let us glimpse what it looks like when God's people worship him wholeheartedly.

But we've still got Nehemiah 13 coming. And it's good that we've still got Nehemiah 13, because we all have to deal even this day with our sinful selves, our imperfect churches, and our messy lives. This side of heaven, we don't get to stay in any one brief, shining moment. Nehemiah is going to leave us longing for and clinging to the Savior who came and finally answered all our sin by bearing it himself and dying for it—the perfect, final sacrifice. In Christ, his Son, God applied the ultimately just and infinitely merciful solution of the cross. All these talks on Nehemiah have sent us finally to the cross, haven't they? There's nowhere to go but to Jesus who died for us, Jesus who rose victorious, Jesus who is coming again.

But let's not forget these chapters. The fact that these people blow it in chapter 13 does not mean we should minimize or leave behind the magnificent worship, the order, and the *joy*. No! These are glimpses, *true* glimpses, of what happens when God's Word works in a people. These are glimpses of what Nehemiah's all about: God's faithfulness to his people, and his call for their faithful response to him. The whole story is not over in Nehemiah's time, but these are glimpses we can hold on to, glimpses that pull our gaze ahead toward what we'll be doing forever as the bride of Christ in that perfectly ordered New Jerusalem.

What will it be like, that city with foundations whose designer and builder is God (Heb. 11:10)? It will be filled with inhabitants who've moved in by grace. It will ring with joyful worship forever (Rev. 5:14; 21:3). And all those there, in perfect order, will cast their crowns before the throne and bring offerings of praise, adoration, and worship (Rev. 4:10–11; 5:9–14).

In Nehemiah, we glimpse that city. In Christ, we take up residence in that city. One day soon, that city is going to come down out of heaven from God (Rev. 21:2). *Amen !*

Reflect and Pray (Parts I, II, and III)

Reflect on each question, and then take a moment to speak or write the prayers that grow from those reflections.

1. There's a lot of joy among God's gathered people in Nehemiah 11–12—growing from all the evidences of God's continuing faithfulness. As those who have received the full revelation of the gospel of Christ, we have been given *even more* evidence of God's faithfulness. Why do you think we are so often not characterized by joy? *were focused on self and temporal worldly things*

2. What's the big deal about joy? Why does it matter that Christians are marked by joy? (If Nehemiah were around today, how might he answer?) *Its evidence of Jesus in us!*

3. God's good work in the midst of his people bears great fruit, including the fruit of lives ordered together according to his Word, growing and worshiping joyfully. Ask God to search and know your heart. Are you living among God's people with a humble and joyful heart? In what specific ways might you more wholeheartedly embrace a life centered around Christ's sacrifice on the cross and resurrection from the dead, a life shared generously with his blood-bought church as it grows and joyfully submits to him?

Help me Jesus

Think Like an Expositor (Part III)

The first question that struck me in reading and observing this concluding section of chapter 12 related to *context*. How does this little paragraph about organizing worship practices follow effectively on the heels of that beautiful worship passage (vv. 27–43)? At first, it seemed a bit of a strange juxtaposition. And how should we take this passage that shows the ordered obedience of God's people in light of the fact that in the next chapter we see all that order disintegrating?

Considering the immediately surrounding texts inevitably drives us to look at the structure and theme of a whole book so as to see where a passage fits into the flow. If this book is about restoration, for example, then we might say it moves (after the introductory chapter) from restoring walls (chaps. 2–6) to restoring people (chaps. 7–12)—all according to God's Word. The second part, about restoring people, moves from a kind of revival around the Word (chaps. 7–10) to the results of that revival in chapters 11–12, the conclusion of which then cements those results—before the *book's* conclusion (chap. 13) "un-cements" them and reminds us that the story of restoration is not over.

The larger biblical and historical context has been well noted by many—both the flow of Old Testament history that leads God's covenant people to this point of restoration after exile, and the flow of this final portion of Old Testament history right toward the Christ promised from their seed, the Christ whose sacrifice will finally put an end to all the temple rituals they are obediently restoring. Considering all the layers of context was crucial in opening up this section and this passage.

I found application of this passage hard at first, but it became increasingly beautiful the more I struggled with it and found it asking me questions about giving myself to the ordered worship of God's people. In fact, it got downright close to home!

7

Leaning Forward
in the Dark:
A Failed Reformation

Nehemiah 13

D. A. Carson

I suppose if I had to give a title to all of Nehemiah, I wouldn't call it *Hand Me Another Brick* or *How to Build a Wall*. It would be something like *The Triumph and Failure of Reformation and Revival*. Moreover, if I were writing the book of Nehemiah—what a cheeky way to put things—in order to turn it into a blockbuster movie, I would end at 12:43, the summary of the spectacular scene of choirs marching in opposite directions around the wall, coming together with glorious orchestral praise in front of the temple: "And on that day they offered great sacrifices, rejoicing because God had given them great joy. The women and children also rejoiced. The sound of rejoicing in Jerusalem could be heard far away."[1] You can picture it: a glorious sunset on the screen with the credits going up and spectacular, exhilarating music in the background. And you go away feeling really good after a couple of hours of escapism in a wonderful film. Instead, the God who gives us this book intends it to end with some administrative commitments (12:44–47) followed by chapter 13, which, on any reading, seems like a bit of a downer.

What has gone wrong? I want, first, to run through the chapter with you, rather quickly, to take in some of the details of this declension, and then to reflect with you on what this is saying about the book of Nehemiah as a whole. Finally, we shall ponder what this says for us when we in our time long for reformation and revival under King Jesus.

A Survey of Nehemiah 13

We must remember that after spending twelve years as governor, Nehemiah returned to serve King Artaxerxes in the palace at Susa. Verse 6 tells us that in the thirty-second year of Artaxerxes's reign, Nehemiah went back to Babylon. He had come in the twentieth year, so he spent twelve years on this complex project of building the wall, repopulating the city, and restoring stability and covenantal fidelity. Back in Susa, Nehemiah apparently returned to his duties in the imperial court. Sometime later—we're not told how long—he seeks permission from the king and returns to Jerusalem, apparently as governor, and what he finds is listed in this chapter.

1. New Legalism (vv. 1–3)

The Book of Moses was read aloud . . . and there it was found written that no Ammonite or Moabite should ever be admitted into the assembly of God, because they had not met the Israel-

[1] Unless otherwise indicated, Scripture references in this chapter are from The Holy Bible, New International Version®, NIV®. Copyright © 1973, 1978, 1984, 2011 by Biblica, Inc.™ Used by permission. All rights reserved worldwide.

ites with food and water but had hired Balaam to call a curse
down on them. (Our God, however, turned the curse into a
blessing.) When the people heard this law, they excluded from
Israel all who were of foreign descent. (Neh. 13:1–3)

When people appear to quote the Bible, it is good to look up the
original text and remind ourselves of the context. One must learn
what the Word of God actually says. In this case, the passage being
referred to is Deuteronomy 23:3–5:

> No Ammonite or Moabite or any of their descendants may
> enter the assembly of the LORD, not even in the tenth genera-
> tion. For they did not come to meet you with bread and water
> on your way when you came out of Egypt, and they hired
> Balaam son of Beor from Pethor in Aram Naharaim to pro-
> nounce a curse on you. However, the LORD your God would
> not listen to Balaam but turned the curse into a blessing for
> you, because the LORD your God loves you.

We need to remember, then, that what God pronounced with
respect to the Moabites and Ammonites arose because of the particular perniciousness with which they sought to corrupt Israel.
Initially, Israel had approached them and said, in effect: "We need
to pass through your territory. We'll pay for any water we drink
and any food we eat." But the Ammonites and Moabites wouldn't
let them through. Eventually, the contest was decided in struggle
and war. Worse than the Ammonites' and Moabites' refusal of a
right of passage, however, was their cynical pursuit of the counsel
of Balaam, a prophet of dubious character. Initially they offered
to pay him well if he would call a curse down on the Israelites—
thinking, perhaps, that because Balaam was some sort of prophet
of Yahweh, he could actually pronounce some incantation or other
that would bring down the wrath of Yahweh on Israel, and thus
their enemies would be destroyed. In the narrative, we learn that
Balaam, though sorely tempted by the money, listens to what God

tells him and manages to muster the courage to avoid pronouncing a curse on God's covenant people.

Sadly, however, the wretched man finds another way to remain in the good graces of the Ammonites and Moabites, and receive some of their money. He counsels them to show themselves friendly, knowing full well what the result will be: their young men and their young women will interact with the young men and young women of Israel, and pretty soon many inter-marriages will take place. The issue, of course, is not the propriety of mixed-race marriages as we think of them; rather, the issue is whether believers should marry unbelievers. To enter into mixed-race marriages will mean that Israel, the covenant people of God, will be intermingling with the surrounding pagans, something God has strictly forbidden. The result will be that God himself will descend on his people with judicial wrath. This is exactly the same sin that Solomon will commit many years later. He will marry many pagan wives, and pretty soon he will fill Jerusalem with pagan temples in order to please his brides. Long before Solomon sinned along these lines, Balaam is already talking to the Ammonites and Moabites and saying, in effect: "If you want God to be angry with the Israelites, don't look to me to provide curses. Just get them to sin. Of course, you must be subtle about it. Don't go out there and say: 'Come on, Israel. Sin. Go ahead and sin.' But go out there and say, 'Isn't my daughter beautiful?' Or, 'My son really loves your daughter.' And pretty soon, in half a generation or so, you will have achieved the same result. You will have people so compromised in their commitment to the living God that they will attract his wrath upon their own heads." But God is not fooled. He is so angered by the seductive wickedness of this sin that he pronounces this curse on Ammon and Moab.

What the people of Judah in Nehemiah 13 infer from this curse goes way beyond anything that Scripture says. The curse was not pronounced with respect to all non-Israelites, but only with respect to the Ammonites and the Moabites. Moreover, the law of God provided ways for most people from the surrounding pagan tribes to join the people of Israel. They could vow allegiance to God, put themselves under the covenant, and accept the covenantal sign of circumcision. They could, in effect, become Israelites. Only the citizens of Ammon and Moab did God prohibit from becoming Israelites, even to the tenth generation. For the people of Nehemiah's day to extend the prohibition to all non-Israelites is to go beyond what God commanded. Their reasoning probably runs something like this: "We see that we are supposed to keep ourselves separate, so we'll *really* separate. We'll expel anybody who claims to be an Israelite today who does not have Abraham's blood coursing through his veins."

This is close to trying to become more holy than God. Moreover, it forgets that God, despite the prohibition, actually set his affection in grace and love on some particular Moabites, such as Ruth, the great-grandmother of David, and she was allowed into the line of the promised Messiah.

The stance the people adopt is something that often recurs in reformations and revivals. Once the movement takes hold, at least some people try to become more holy than God. When I was an undergraduate at McGill University many moons ago, the Christian fellowship group of which I was a part was constantly interacting with Marxists. It was, after all, the 1960s. Thousands of students went around the campus carrying Mao Tse-tung's *Little Red Book*. I carefully read it myself from cover to cover. I'm sure there were times when it was in the stack of books I was carrying, too. There were a lot of *Little Red Books* on the campus. One of the Christian leaders suggested that we Christians ought to start carrying our Bibles: "If the Marxists are pleased to carry Mao's *Little Red Book* as a badge of honor, shouldn't we be grateful to God for the book that God has given us? So, start carrying Bibles." Pretty soon, many Christians in McGill Christian Fellowship started carrying Bibles. Several weeks later, however, I noticed that some of my fellow Christians were carrying very big, black Bibles.

It is very easy somehow to turn what is a good instinct, even a biblically prescribed mandate, into something that is not only rule-oriented but also a kind of public display attesting that I am one of the good guys. That conduct is a little rare as long as the reformation is unpopular, but once the reformation takes hold, then almost inevitably some people try to be more holy than God. Strictly speaking, they are less interested in listening carefully to what God's Word says than in gaining a reputation for godliness. And this, of course, is a form of legalism. Instead of casting themselves on the mercy of God, they start surrounding themselves with endless rules that they can always justify in some way or other by appealing loosely to something or other in the Bible. But the authority of the Bible somehow gets trumped by external rules that go several steps beyond what the Bible says. For example, instead of following Sabbath law, we may create thirty-nine categories of prohibited work that are meant to codify proper practice, but which go beyond what God says—and this, of course, was the practice of the rabbis in Jesus's day—a new legalism.

2. The Triumph of Nepotism (vv. 4–9)

Blood relations became more important than the blood of the covenant. Do you see what happens in Nehemiah 13:4–9? "Eliashib the priest had been put in charge of the storerooms of the house of our God. He was closely associated with Tobiah" (v. 4). The words "was closely associated with" translate a Hebrew idiom that probably means the two men are tied to each other by marriage bonds in their extended families. Because of this family connection, using his power as the one in charge of the storerooms in the temple, Eliashib clears out a suite of rooms to make a nice apartment for Tobiah—the Tobiah who had sneered when the wall was being built: "Hah! Stupid little wall! If a fox jumps up on it, it will crumble" (cf. 4:3). Archaeology has exposed that wall. At the top, it is about nine feet across—strong enough and big enough to support two choirs solemnly parading around the perimeter of the city, singing back and forth antiphonally, complete with accompanying orchestras. Some fox!

This Tobiah, having lost his bid to prevent the restoration of Jerusalem, now wants to be on the winning side, the side where the money is, where the power is. Jerusalem had been a pile of ruins. Now it is beginning to become a prosperous place, and he would like to have his own business apartment downtown, right at the center. The temple complex would do fine, don't you think? So Eliashib cleans out some of the rooms—rooms that are supposed to be storing the utensils and products necessary for the right operation of the temple. This is simultaneously despising the temple of God and colluding with the enemy as if the holiness of God doesn't matter. Nepotism is more important than the covenant. A blood relation is more important than the blood of the covenant.

I could tell you the story of a particular seminary where the president worried about the theological drift of his son. He knew that his son no longer held to inerrancy. But he persuaded the faculty members of that seminary to take this son on as a faculty member in the hope, no doubt, that somehow the strength of the other faculty members would rein him in a little bit and straighten him out. In fact, this became one of the first steps toward that seminary's drift in another direction. That seminary president would not have done that for my son. He did it for his own son. The name of the game is nepotism.

It is small wonder that Jesus insists that we are to love God more than our own parents (Matt. 10:37). In fact, he could put it in the strongest sort of rhetoric, an opposition that is initially shocking to us—the one who loves Jesus must *hate* his father and mother (Luke 14:26). This is, of course, a way of speaking in absolute terms to get a point across. The same Bible teaches us that we are to honor our parents. And yet, when it comes to competing claims of allegiance to Jesus and allegiance to bloodlines, allegiance to Jesus must win. But here in Nehemiah 13, nepotism triumphs over faithfulness to God.

3. The Neglect of Covenantal Faithfulness, Especially with Respect to the Temple (vv. 10-13)

There are some parts of Nehemiah we have not spent a lot of time on. We have jumped over them rather quickly, but they are surfacing again here. For example, in the renewal of the covenant in chapter 10, what is striking is that most of the vows are bound up with the temple. You and I might think: "Why in their renewal of the covenant did they not devote space to stipulating morality? to prohibiting idolatry? to emphasizing the importance of telling the truth and loving God with heart and soul and mind and strength, and not committing adultery and not succumbing to hate?" None of those things is mentioned in the covenant renewal of Nehemiah 10. There is a generalized mandate to obey all of the Law of Moses, but then almost all of the rest of the terms of the covenant renewal focus on allegiance to the ceremonial aspects of the Law that provide for the flourishing of the temple. We might even be tempted to think: "Was Nehemiah some sort of a pre-Jesus Pharisee, a man primarily interested in the externals of religion? Is that the way we are supposed to understand him?"

No, of course not. The temple was central in the covenant-renewal ceremony of Nehemiah 10 precisely because the relationship between us and God—between human beings and God—is more important than relationships among ourselves. Obviously one dare not put a wedge between the two, as if it is possible to develop one relationship and not the other. But the sad reality is this: today, when we think of sin, we often think almost exclusively in terms of social malformations and aberrations of one sort or another, not of offense against God.

Do you ever wake up in the middle of the night and, in that half-luminescent waking-sleeping moment, find your mind flashing back to something shameful that you've done in the past? Perhaps you recall something extraordinarily stupid, insensitive, or cruel that you've said, and you sort of writhe there in the sheets for a few moments, wishing that you could go back and redo that bit of your life. But, of course, "The moving hand having writ moves on," as the poet says. You can't go back. Soon, mercifully, you fall asleep again. Tell me this: when you writhe there in shame for a few moments in this half-asleep, half-awake interlude, before whom are you feeling shame? Isn't it virtually always before other people? "I can't believe I embarrassed myself by saying something so stupid." Why are we not ashamed before God? Is it not because we primarily think of sin on the horizontal plane, and not with reference to God? But sin is first and foremost offense against God (Ps. 51:4). So how come we don't wake up and writhe in embarrassment over our sins before God?

But Nehemiah gets it. Yes, in the renewal of the covenant, there must be vows of commitment to obey the whole law. But Nehemiah understands that what we must have, above all else, is a right relationship with God. Under the terms of the old covenant, that relationship was secured by the sacrifices in the temple that God himself had ordained. Of course, we know that such sacrifices pointed forward to the ultimate temple, to the ultimate sacrifice, to the ultimate Passover Lamb. We know that. But at Nehemiah's point in redemptive history, the access God's people have to forgiveness, to reconciliation with God, is precisely through the temple structures that God himself ordained. And that is why there is so much emphasis on the temple right through this book. This is why, after the beautiful scene with the credits running up the screen (up to 12:43), you have the institutionalization of order to make sure that the temple sacrificial system is preserved (12:44–47).

So what do we find in this time of spiritual declension? We find the sad neglect of covenantal faithfulness, especially with respect to the temple. The wood is not being gathered, no one is providing the needed sacrificial animals, the rota system has lapsed, and people are no longer supporting the choirs or the priests and Levites, with the result that they have to support themselves and the temple system is collapsing. In each case, Nehemiah takes strong action to clean up the problem. He is right to take these steps. But what does the failure itself say about how deeply this reformation and revival have taken hold?

4. The Triumph of Profit over Piety (vv. 15-22)

If you can make a little extra money on the Sabbath, then why observe the Sabbath? Once again, the action that Nehemiah takes is pretty rigorous. He is right to adopt this course. But what does it say about the status of the reformation?

5. Mixed Marriages (vv. 23-28)

Despite the stringent separation found in the opening verses of this chapter, we now discover that the problem of mixed marriages has nevertheless returned (vv. 23–28). Ezra faced that a decade and a half earlier. Solomon faced it five centuries earlier. Three or four centuries before that, in part because of the advice of Balaam, the Israelites faced it with respect to Ammon and Moab. Now the challenge of covenantal faithlessness has reared its head again. One can imagine the cries: "But I love him!" or "I know a Christian woman who married a non-Christian guy and he was converted, you know, after three years. It worked out very well for them, you know."

When Nehemiah comments that some of their kids can't even speak Aramaic, but can communicate only in some dialect of Ammonite, he is not inciting xenophobia, a hatred of strangers, a kind of narrow tribalism. The point is that these children do not know the language of the people of God, so they do not know the covenants of the people of God, they do not know the worship of the people of God, they do not know the Word of God, and they do not know the God of the people of God. Doubtless in retrospect, some are muttering piously, "That Israelite religion is a bit narrow, you know; I don't go for that" or "I'm quite a spiritual person, and I find the religion of the Ammonites deeply meaningful." This kind of declension has reached all the way up to the high priest's family: "One of the sons of Joiada son of Eliashib the high priest was son-in-law to Sanballat the Horonite. And I drove him away" (v. 28).

6. The Spiritual Declension of Nehemiah's Prayer

There is one more possible mark of declension in this chapter, though I confess I am not totally sure of it. Have you noticed that at two or three points in the book, Nehemiah has said something like, "Remember me, O God, for what I have done"? The first such utterance shows up in 5:19: "Remember me with favor, my God, for all I have done for these people." And, of course, similar words keep showing up in this thirteenth chapter: "Remember me for this, my God, and do not blot out what I have so faithfully done for the house of my God and its services" (v. 14); "Remember me for this also, my God, and show mercy to me according to your great love" (v. 22b); "Remember them, my God, because they defiled the priestly office and the covenant of the priesthood and of the Levites" (v. 29). And, then, how does the book end up? "Remember me with favor, my God" (v. 31).

Now, if we were to find only one of these verses, it would be easy to make sense of it as the faithful utterance of a godly man looking into the face of his heavenly Father. It would be a kind of Old Testament analog to what the apostle Paul says in 2 Timothy: "I have fought the good fight, I have finished the race, I have kept the faith. Now there is in store for me the crown of righteousness, which the Lord, the righteous Judge, will award to me on that day" (4:7–8a). Nehemiah's utterances sound roughly equivalent to that, don't they? But when they show up in this degree of concentration in the last chapter, where all the paragraphs are about spiritual declension, another overtone can be heard. This does not sound exactly like the Nehemiah of chapter 1—the Nehemiah who says: "I confess the sins we Israelites, including myself and my father's family, have committed against you. We have acted very wickedly toward you. We have not obeyed the commands, decrees and laws you gave your servant Moses. Remember the instruction you gave your servant Moses, saying, 'If you are unfaithful, I will scatter you among the nations'" (vv. 6–8). Another "remember" is embedded here, of course, but it is a "remember" that calls God to keep in mind his covenantal mercy even when the people are sinning: "'If you return to me and obey my commands, then, even if your exiled people are at the farthest horizon, I will gather them from there and bring them to the place I have chosen as a dwelling for my Name.' They are your servants and your people, whom you redeemed by your great strength and your mighty hand. Lord, let your ear be attentive to the prayer of this your servant and to the prayer of your servants who delight in revering your name" (vv. 9–11a).

Why doesn't this book end up with: "Remember, O Lord, so to work within us by your power according to your covenantal mercies, that we will again revere your name"? Why do we get this repeated refrain in this chapter: "Remember me, Lord, because I've done quite a lot of work. I've done a pretty good job. I mean, they failed. Remember them, too, for the bad things they've done. But remember me for the good things I've done"? In other words, this feels like a kind of spiritual declension, a slightly disappointing focus on self, with overtones of self-exoneration.

That might be too harsh. Doubtless God will pronounce his own verdict on the last day; he will sort this one out. But I do ask myself why God in his perfect wisdom has recorded four of these utterances in one short chapter, the last chapter, a chapter that conveys a tone and emphasis rather different from the rest of the book, and certainly very different from what we find on Nehemiah's lips in the first chapter.

That is how the reformation ends. That is how the book ends.

There are some people who are used by God to bring along the church of the living God in some wonderfully powerful ways for a period of time, but who end up, late in life, destroying what they built. This may happen for a lot of reasons. Some people get cranky. They discover at seventy-five that they cannot do what they did at forty-five, and they resent the younger folk who are fol-lowing them. Wittingly or otherwise, they begin to destroy what they built.

A number of years ago at Trinity Evangelical Divinity School, we invited Carl F. H. Henry and Kenneth Kantzer, then in their eighties, to give lectures on their perception of evangelicalism and its health (or otherwise!) in the United States during the previous century. The lives of these men had been closely intertwined with many of the major movements during that time. Now, in their senior years, they graciously accepted our invitation to lecture to our entire student body about what God had done in their understanding and experience. The lectures were informed and interesting. The next day, I was charged with interviewing them before the same student body. I didn't tell them the questions in advance. Most of the questions were straightforward, and, as one might have expected, they always answered with sagacity, nuance, and maturity. They were old hands at answering questions, of course. Finally, I asked this question: "When they get old, some men become defensive, crotchety, and mean-spirited. They're al-ways looking backward; they are resentful of the young. But you two, as you've gotten older, have become more generous. You are constantly looking to the future. You constantly provide en-couragement to young men and women coming along behind; you pray with the future in view, and you thank God for the past. I do not detect any root of bitterness in you, any malice or grumpiness. How did that happen? Don't tell me it's the grace of God; I know it's the grace of God. I want to know how the grace of God so worked in your life that this is how you have come to look at things at the end of your lives. Can you articulate that?" They both sputtered a little—two very articulate men not know-ing what to say and looking like deer caught in headlights. Finally, Carl Henry quietly mumbled the best moment of those hours of videotaping. He said, "How can anyone be arrogant when he stands beside the cross?"

What we miss at the end of Nehemiah is some sort of utterance as this: "How can anyone be arrogant or self-justified when he looks back over the last two or three decades and sees what God has done to transform this city and to anticipate the coming of the promised Redeemer?" What we hear instead is: "Remember me, O God, because I've done a pretty good job. I've worked pretty hard."

What Nehemiah Is About

So what shall we make of Nehemiah 13, and of this entire book? What do we learn from it? This seems to be a rather depressing way to end a conference, let alone a book, doesn't it?

Some people say that the lesson we should derive from Nehemiah is basically this: there's sin at the beginning, there's sin in the middle, and there's sin at the end. Because all this takes place under the old covenant, that is all there is: sin at the beginning, sin in the middle, and sin at the end. You just have to wait for Jesus.

There is at least some truth to this reading. That is why the exposition of John Piper in this volume is so telling. Again and again, we stumble across these cycles of sin that take down the people of God. Then, in line with Piper's six polarities of judgment, we trace the cries to God for mercy, and God responding in mercy, before the wretched cycle starts all over again.

Indeed, it is possible to drill down and uncover the same pattern in a micro way, in smaller historical contexts. For example, after reading the blessings and curses of the book of Deuteronomy, what do we find at the end of Deuteronomy? We discover that Moses himself does not get into the Promised Land. Forty years later, the Israelites do enter the land, of course, but then we read the cycles of the book of Judges: a generation or two, and the people succumb to idolatry again and again. Judgment falls: the Midianites are upon them, the Philistines are upon them. God raises up a hero, a judge of some sort, and the foreign troops are cleared out again. Sadly, however, each cycle goes a little lower into moral slime, all the way to the end of the book of Judges, when everyone does that which is right in his own eyes. The moral quagmire is so ghastly that even the so-called "good guys" are morally appalling people. It is difficult to read Judges 19–21 in polite company. It's horrible stuff—you cut your concubine into parts and send the parts around Israel to gather the nation to fight? These are the good guys! "O God, how we need a king to impose order and civility!" So the people get a king—but Saul does not work out too well. So God raises up his own king, a man after his own heart, and it is not long before David commits adultery and murder. One wonders what he would have done if he hadn't been a man after God's own heart. The succeeding narratives do not become any more hopeful.

So there is a sense in which Nehemiah is simply part of the Old Testament storyline that keeps saying there's sin at the beginning, there's sin in the middle, and there's sin at the end. There is no answer here. We must await the ultimate King, the ultimate Priest, the ultimate temple, the ultimate sacrifice. We must await Jesus himself, who bears our sin once for all—Jesus the ultimate King and temple, the ultimate meeting place between God and sinners.

Moreover, there is another failure lurking in the silences of this book. Recall that Jerusalem itself is symbol-laden. Jerusalem is the city of the Great King, the place of the temple, where God has chosen to plant his name. Under the terms of the old covenant, Jerusalem is the center of the covenant people of God. In particular, it is the city of the throne of the Davidic dynasty. In the previous chapter, Jenny Salt and Kathleen Nielson pointed out the repeated references to David in Nehemiah 12. Mention of David inevitably raises an important question, for something is missing. We now have the people in Jerusalem; we have the temple; we have the priests; we have the sacrificial system. All of this is pretty wonderful. But where is David? To mention David in chapter 12 reminds us that, for this nation to be properly constituted, there needs to be an heir to the promised Davidic line. Politically, of course, that isn't possible in Nehemiah's time. Any Davidic claimant, restored to the throne, would bring down all of the forces of Persia, the regional superpower, onto the head of this little city-state. The Israelites know who the Davidic king should be, for the genealogical records have been preserved. But the reformation led by Nehemiah remains incomplete without the son of David. And now, in chapter 13 the reformation seems to be frittering itself away.

At what point in the unfolding of history would it be possible to set on the throne someone in the Davidic line? What takes place after the Old Testament books are no longer being written? It is easy to summarize these developments. The Persian Empire is taken over by the Greek Empire. Alexander the Great and his marauding forces extend the empire all the way to the borders of India. And then, still in his thirties, Alexander dies. He bequeaths his kingdom to four generals. One of them establishes the Seleucid dynasty just to the north of Israel, in Syria. Another establishes the Ptolemaic dynasty to the south of Israel, in Egypt. That means little Israel is squashed in no man's land, unable to achieve independence, perpetually under the thumb of one power or the other. Certainly Israel cannot be allowed to have its own king, a Davidic king. Eventually, at the beginning of the second century BC, one of the Seleucid kings decides that he is going to crush Judaism once and for all. He moves in his troops, sacrifices pigs in the temple, and makes it a capital offense to observe the Sabbath or to own any part of the Law. He resolves to kill all priests. But God raises up a guerrilla warrior nicknamed Judas the Hammer—in Aramaic, Judas Maccabeus, and hence, the Maccabean revolt. The Maccabeans excel in guerrilla warfare. After three and a half years of bloody skirmishes, they build up enough strength to have a set battle with the Syrians on the banks of the Orontes River, where they thoroughly defeat the Syrian army.

For the first time in half a millennium, these Judeans are free to appoint a scion of David to the throne in Jerusalem. You might think that they would be saying, in effect: "At last, we can restore

Jerusalem, the city of God, to its God-ordained role. Now we may delight in the temple that brings sinful men and women into the presence of God, in the God-ordained priesthood that mediates between God and sinful human beings, in God-ordained sacrifices that cover our sins—and now also in the restoration of the God-ordained Davidic dynasty." And thus they would be preparing the way for the ultimate Davidic King, the one who is called by Isaiah, centuries earlier, "the Mighty God, the Everlasting Father, the Prince of Peace" (Isa. 9:6).

That, surely, is what we might expect. But what do these guerilla leaders actually do? They simply seize power for themselves. Another century goes by. We arrive at 63 BC, and the growing Roman Empire takes over. The Romans appoint their own puppet king in the person of Herod.

And where is David? Where are the promises of God? We leaf through a few more pages in our Bibles and we read in the first line of the New Testament: "This is the genealogy of Jesus the Messiah the son of *David*, the son of Abraham" (Matt. 1:1). The ultimate King has come; the ultimate Priest has come; the ultimate temple has come; the ultimate sacrifice has come; and the New Jerusalem is right around the corner. So until the dawning of these great events, still four centuries beyond Nehemiah, surely there is some sense in which the book that bears his name really is saying, with brutal realism, that there is sin at the beginning, there is sin in the middle, and there is sin at the end.

Yet with a little more reflection, we perceive that we must say more than this. After all, much was accomplished in the short term. We dare not despise days of reformation and revival. The wonderful fact of the matter is that the people of God experienced genuine renewal. In the book of Nehemiah, the Jerusalem wall is rebuilt. The city is repopulated. The sacrificial system is restored. There are moments of great public confession, moving tears, the sense of the presence of God powerfully experienced among them. It is a great time of personal and national revival. It should not be despised just because it comes to an end. After all, in a similar way, although we would not want to underestimate the power of Christ and the gospel, that gospel is not yet consummated in our day. The result is that even though we live on this side of the cross, even though there is no more sacrifice for sin because the ultimate sacrifice has been paid, even though the Davidic king is now reigning with all authority in heaven and on earth, nevertheless the consummation has not yet dawned. The result is that his blood-bought church, like the covenant people of old, experiences times of reformation and revival, *and* times of declension. Is it adequate to say nothing more than that, in the history of the church, there is sin at the beginning, sin in the middle, and sin at the end, when God sends times of reformation and revival that he uses to stabilize the faith of countless thousands, and that frequently serve as a springboard for fruitful evangelism and stunning growth?

The cycles of revival and declension in the life of the church start within the pages of the New Testament itself. For examples of declension, one might read the letters to the seven churches in Revelation 2 and 3. Five of the seven churches are in danger of having their candlesticks removed—that is, they will stop being churches unless they repent. God will snuff out their light. They will not be the people of God anymore. God holds his new-covenant people accountable for fidelity, even as he held his old-covenant people accountable. Indeed, the general tone of the New Testament is that we have so much more light than our Old Testament brothers and sisters in God that we are in greater danger if we ignore this revelation. Hence, for example: "Therefore we must pay much closer attention to what we have heard, lest we drift away from it. For since the message declared by angels proved to be reliable, and every transgression or disobedience received a just retribution, how shall we escape if we neglect such a great salvation?" (Heb. 2:1–3a ESV).

It pleased God to raise up Nehemiah and Ezra, and to bring in times of massive restoration, with good effects that trailed on for centuries, even though sin was not slow to raise its head and contest the ground that was gained. Similarly, it has pleased God to send times of genuine reformation and revival in the life of the church, with good effects that have trailed on for centuries, even though sin has not been slow to raise its head and contest the triumph of the gospel. Until Christ returns, we will see more of both reformation and declension. In the pattern of the experience of Old Testament saints, it will please God to pour out yet more blessings on his blood-bought church—but there will also be times of failure in the church of the living God. That the struggle continues until the consummation cannot be allowed to dampen our enthusiastic hope that God in grace will pour out his Spirit in yet greater reformation and revival. Is there not something in you which, as you read accounts of reformation and revival, both in Scripture and in the history of the church, cries out with brothers and sisters around the world: "O Lord God, do it again! Do it again!"

Reflections for Our World

I have been on the edges of revival in two or three places. I shall mention one of them, the so-called Canadian revival in 1970. It began with the preaching ministry of the Sutera twins in Saskatoon, Saskatchewan. What started off as some brief meetings turned into ongoing meetings night after night as the praises of God filled the building, men and women confessed their sin, and people came in off the street not quite knowing why they were there, yet soon fell under deep conviction of sin and were converted. The crime rate in the city fell as people restored things they had stolen. The movement soon spread across much of the country. However, sad to relate, it quickly dissipated and died. Who is wise enough to explain all the dynamics of the dissipation? But I remember hearing one spectacular story, as a Christian publicly confessed his sin, of how the Lord had restored him to a right relationship with God. God granted to this man a clear understanding of the ugly idolatries in his life and a renewed grasp of the love of God poured out on the cross. He was simultaneously ashamed and grateful, crushed and released, aware of the depth of his sin and the infinitely greater depth of grace. Tears flowed down his face, and no one could tell which tears signaled abject sorrow and which tears signaled holy joy. It was so very moving. Unfortunately, that story, among many others that started off with spontaneous gratitude and adoration, soon became part of organized storytelling so that others might "catch" the revival. Two or three Christian leaders took it on themselves to fly this man around the country so he could retell the story. Soon the spontaneity and authenticity were diminished. In the effort to keep the movement alive, Christians tried to domesticate and control what only God can do.

The sad truth is that in times of declension, we soon find merely organized piety. Strange to tell, one can find pseudo-pious legalism and ugly disobedience in the same crowd—just what we find in Nehemiah 13. Worse, we may begin to pant after spiritual experiences without panting after God.

Yet we must not come to the end of Nehemiah and conclude on a note of fatalism: "If God sends revival, God sends revival. There's nothing I can do about it. If he withholds revival, he withholds revival. There's nothing I can do about it." Rather, we must follow the pattern already set down in the old-covenant Scriptures, the pattern that insists we examine ourselves before the living God, confess our sins, and plead for mercy. True, God brings judgment; God also brings reformation and revival. Who knows what he will do for us in our time? Is he not our holy, loving, heavenly, and gracious Father?

So we press on, constantly aware that Christ has said, "I will build my church, and the gates of Hades will not overcome it." We cannot be certain whether God will visit us with more judgment, as we deserve in the Western world, or visit us with great mercy and transforming power. But even if God in his grace were to send reforming and reviving fire among us in our time, understand this:

unless Jesus should come back right in the middle of it, there will be further periods of declension. Nevertheless, the blessings of reformation and revival will trail on, a glorious anticipation of the new heaven and the new earth, where we will see God as he is. The struggles will continue until the end of the age, when Jesus will crush the last enemy, death itself. Until then, God will continue to speak to his people through the words of Nehemiah, holding up before us the glory of reformation and revival while calling us to perseverance when its glories start to fade. God's people will always take the long view that anticipates the glory around the throne, while even now we petition that throne for reformation and revival such as we have not known in our time.

Reflect and Pray

Reflect on each question, and then take a moment to speak or write the prayers that grow from those reflections.

1. What stands out to you most about how God's people declined in Nehemiah 13, and why? In what ways do you find similar declension happening today within the church?
2. In one sentence, summarize how the book of Nehemiah anticipates and prepares for the coming of Jesus Christ. In another sentence, summarize how the events recorded in this book strengthen us as we wait for his second coming.
3. Identify three or four insights about God's character and the character of his salvation the Lord has granted you through your study of Nehemiah. Write a prayer of praise to the Lord, shaped by these insights. Who in your life needs to hear these truths about God? How might God use you to share with others the riches you have seen in his Word?

Think Like an Expositor

The conclusion to Nehemiah is a hard one. Don Carson's comments on his preparation suggest in general the wisdom of

[Handwritten marginalia:]
- *Nehemiah asked God to "remember his goodness" his PRIDE*
- *It demonstrates the inadequacy of the law to change people*
- *The people became lazy + did things their own way. They compromised + did what made sense to them*
- *The Lord is the same yesterday today tomorrow. He is unchanging and faithful to his plans + will.*

working not just on topics and passages in our teaching series, but on whole books—in the form in which God gave them to us. Surely it makes sense that the end makes sense most clearly in light of all that comes before:

> I'm not sure that my experience of preparing this chapter was typical, in that I had already preached through the entire book. In other words, when I prepared for chapter 13, I did so after preparing for chapters 1–12. It is so much easier to prepare to preach the last chapter after preaching through all the other chapters! It also meant that I was keeping an eye peeled for how this chapter brought the book to a close.

His comments conclude soberly, which seems appropriate for the book of Nehemiah. He would remind us of the seriousness of letting the text speak clearly:

> One of the things that expository preaching must do, especially in narrative texts and discourse texts, is unpack *the flow* of the thought. That means that ideally the structure of the sermon, or of a large part of the sermon, will reflect the structure of the text itself. If sermons fasten on relatively small details in the text, and congregate everything around those details by imposing an alien structure, then even though everything included in the sermon may be true, hearers will find it more difficult to follow the flow of the argument in the text itself. And that's a serious loss.

Conclusion

On Old Testament Narrative

Kathleen Nielson

This book began with a discussion of biblical exposition; it has moved through a series of biblical expositions on one Old Testament narrative, with added reflection questions and commentary; now, in conclusion, it seems appropriate to look back and comment on this particular genre we've explored in the book of Nehemiah, with the hope that many will be encouraged to study and teach it with increasing delight and effectiveness. God obviously considered narrative a worthy means of communication for his inspired Word. The Old Testament stories are a great gift to be relished—and to be expounded by faithful teachers and preachers.

As with the introductory remarks, these comments will be brief. I recommend further reading of the authors and books noted, in order to dig deeper into the Bible's narratives.

Old Testament Narrative Is Story

This fact that narrative is story is obvious and basic, but we should notice it—and delight in it. Scripture's stories are not a decorative shell for theological truth; they are the revelation of God to us, in all the details of their "storyness." Old Testament narratives are true stories, to be sure; these stories give us the real, live history of our faith, telling us what actually happened, generation after generation. But these true stories are shaped, selective, and full of artistry—great gifts from a Creator God.

Stories are universal. By that I mean that people throughout human history and throughout the diverse cultures of the world all tell stories in one way or another. In fact, one profitable way to study the history of any civilization is to study its stories. That the impulse to create and relish stories transcends culture must be one reason God amply filled with story this Word that he purposed to send out to all the nations. As we consider the genre of narrative, we should remember that its beauties (and all the Bible's literary beauties) are part of God's gracious means not just to grow and nourish believers, but also to draw new believers to himself. I've seen many a woman come to a Bible study and be drawn into the details and the power of a story she doesn't yet understand, but which somehow moves her and connects with her.

Stories do tend to draw people—all kinds of people. Is there anyone reading this who has not been asked by a child, "Tell me a story"? But why do people love stories? Perhaps it's because God made us human beings to live in place and time and flesh and blood—which is where stories happen. We're all living out stories, seeing them unfold, waiting for the end! We all recognize and resonate with universal themes that stories treat, themes of beginnings, endings, birth and death, family, hope, grief, love, loss, good vs. evil, seasons and harvests, longing for home, and on and on.[1]

I find it fascinating that my preschool granddaughter regularly asks to have this or that event in her life recounted by an omniscient narrator (me), with herself as the third-person heroine. Events that involve discipline are popular requests. "Tell it to me

[1] Leland Ryken offers a helpful discussion of "Master Images and Archetypes" in biblical literature in *Words of Delight: A Literary Introduction to the Bible* (Grand Rapids, MI: Baker, 1987), 25–29. This book includes an extensive section on biblical narrative.

in a story," says Adelyn. And so I begin: "Late one afternoon, Adelyn went into the kitchen, smelled and then glimpsed the yummy chocolate cookies on the counter, glanced around, and saw that no one was watching . . ." It's not like she doesn't know what's going to happen! But she's transfixed by her story. I think all of us human beings are transfixed by our stories.

Stories are concrete. One of the distinguishing features of narrative is that it invites us into concrete experience, not just abstract idea. Often we think of the apostle Paul's theological propositions as the Bible's real, hard stuff, and story and poetry as the more ethereal fluff. Actually, theological propositions, crucial as they are, can be pretty abstract and heady—whereas story deals with stuff like feasts with lots of food and drink, broken-down walls, women getting pregnant, battles and blood, sheep, bread, and all of the physical reality where we live and where God is working moment by moment.

Many of us have observed (or used to *be*) giggling young readers who found and marked certain very graphic parts of the Bible that are fun to read—again and again. How about that story in Judges 3 of Ehud thrusting his sword into the very fat belly of King Eglon? In vivid detail, the text says the hilt went in after the blade, and the fat closed over the blade—and that's not all it says! Scripture's narratives are remarkably concrete, and that's the nature of story: to give us real experience in a concrete place and time.

The scene from Nehemiah 2, in which sad-faced Nehemiah serves wine to the Persian king, Artaxerxes (with the queen sitting right beside him, we're told), ushers us right into the tension of that particular moment in the presence of royalty—which contrasts starkly with the later scene from that same chapter, in which Nehemiah, safely in Jerusalem, rides out at night "by the Valley Gate to the Dragon Spring and to the Dung Gate" to inspect the broken-down walls and fire-destroyed gates (v. 13). We may not know exactly where each named gate, spring, and pool was located, but as Nehemiah rides past them one by one, we are transported along with him in this memorable nighttime inspection tour, passing burned-down gate after burned-down gate, along the rubble of Jerusalem's wall. The scene feels both surreal and desolately real.

These concrete stories fill the Scriptures. They are our history as God's people, and God is gracious to "tell it to us in a story." Over a third of the Old Testament comes to us in narrative form, giving us salvation history through the true stories of real people who lived it out. God clearly wants us to pay close attention to the details of these stories; they're definitely not just for the children! Steven Mathewson comments that "many churches teach Bible stories to children downstairs in the basement while the adults study Paul's epistles upstairs in the auditorium."[2] No—we all need to hear these stories that fill the Scriptures, and we need to hear them taught. Even as we receive them and delight in them in the narrative form God inspired, we must remember that they are true and that their truth instructs us. As John Piper reminded us in chapter 5:

> There is a point to the narrative—and the point is a person. Biblical stories are no more ends in themselves than history is an end in itself or the universe is an end in itself. The universe is telling the glory of God (Ps. 19:1). And the history of the world is what it is to show that God is who he is. God writes the story of history to reveal who he is—what he is like, his character, his name.

Asking Questions about Old Testament Narratives

There is no set formula for approaching Old Testament narrative. Sometimes we think there must be some special route, known only to scholars, that leads into the deep meaning of these stories—a special key that unlocks this genre. In his wonderful little book on Old Testament narrative, Dale Ralph Davis explains that this isn't so:

> I think sometimes we can have—or give—the impression that there is a smoke-filled room hidden away somewhere in the

---

[2] Steven D. Mathewson, *The Art of Preaching Old Testament Narrative* (Grand Rapids, MI: Baker, 2002), 23.

Palace of Biblical Interpretation where a few hermeneutical high priests parcel out the secrets for *really* understanding Scripture, especially the Od Testament. Of course, this is simply mental mythology.[3]

Davis goes on, then, to suggest some questions to ask of texts, and to offer some examples of dealing with particular texts and narrative issues. Indeed, asking basic questions is just what we need to do in order to understand and then expound a story. I will suggest six.

What Can I Observe?

This question is the starting point for studying a text of any kind; it represents an initial openness to praying, reading, rereading, and listening well to God's voice in these living and active words. We saw this starting point recommended by a number of the contributors, and all of them no doubt would affirm the need to begin by listening well to a text before trying to do something with it. The whole process begins with listening to God in prayer and asking him to open our ears to hear his voice in his Word, by his Spirit. When we approach study of the text with focused prayer, then turning to the text itself seems not so much an academic-flavored interruption of communion with God as a continuation of listening and responding to his voice.

The first step in observation is to read the entire book, so that from the start we have a sense of the whole and are able to discern just how any one section of text fits in. Some complete books are amazingly compact narratives—Esther, for example, which asks to be processed as one unified, intricately shaped narrative unit. The story of Joseph is one long narrative within the book of Genesis (chaps. 37–50)[4]; we can study and teach smaller episodes in

---

[3] Dale Ralph Davis, *The Word Became Fresh: How to Preach from Old Testament Narrative Texts* (Ross-shire, Scotland: Christian Focus, 2009), 2–3.
[4] Genesis 38 feels like an interruption in this long narrative, but it's not; the story of Judah and Tamar is strategically placed between the chapter in which Joseph is sold into Egypt (37) and the

his story, but observation must begin with the whole flow of his narrative and of the book in which it is placed. We'll get to the importance of context; this is the groundwork. The wall-building episodes in the first part of Nehemiah lead into the people-building episodes in the second part; we must start by following Nehemiah from beginning to end.

When we approach a particular text, then, what should we look to observe? It's helpful to have the text printed out so that we can mark it up as we read and read again. Each text tells us what it wants us to notice, in a sense—and each text we study helps us study the next one better (and the previous ones better next time!). In a narrative, repeated words and phrases often stand out; we want to mark those and watch to see if they lead to important themes, or perhaps sections of the story. For example, Nehemiah mentions God's hand several times in the first couple of chapters; clearly, he is presenting his story as part of God's sovereign direction of the history of his called-out people—from the time of Moses, when God's strong hand redeemed them (1:10), to this present moment, when God's good hand is upon Nehemiah as he makes his request to the king (2:8). It makes a difference to notice this from the start.

Sometimes we notice puzzling or surprising things, and we can mark them and come back to them. Why, for example, in the midst of the crisis that begins the book, does Nehemiah stop and insert such a long prayer? Why does he wait until the very end of chapter 1 to introduce himself as cupbearer to the king?

One helpful way to begin observation of a story is to use the three commonly accepted elements of narrative: characters, setting, and plot—which I usually observe in the order in which they attract my attention in a particular story. Sometimes there's a complex list of characters to write down and keep track of—and often there are contrasting or parallel characters to note. Sometimes we see a character develop. Sometimes, as is the case in Nehemiah,

---

chapter on Joseph and Potiphar's wife (39)—shedding light in both directions, especially by contrast. This is part of what we need to observe in the text!

there's a clear central character. It's always important to watch just how a character is revealed to us by the narrator—and, of course, in the case of Nehemiah, the narrator and the main character are one and the same. As a result, we get to know the thoughts and feelings of Nehemiah a bit better than we do those of most characters; most Old Testament characters are not described by the narrator in any detail, inside or outside! This makes the case of Nehemiah extra interesting: What does Nehemiah want us to know about him, and why?

In Old Testament narrative, the setting is often sketched with a quick hand—a field, a tent, or a mountain. We don't get many details—although, when we do, we should watch. The setting of Ruth moves from foreignness and emptiness to a rich home and harvest fullness, all of which mirrors the whole movement of the book—and the full provision of God. The royal setting of Esther is as fancy and intricate as the plot. The ultimate place, of course, is the place of blessing where God dwells with his people—a place lost in Eden and longed for ever since. In Nehemiah, the holy city of Jerusalem with its temple is the crucial place, the place of promise to which the faithful remnant has returned, the place of worship and reinstituted sacrifice for those who will now wait to see how God will fulfill his promises of salvation and blessing. Asking from the start why this place is so important to Nehemiah can help us discern an important key to the book.

The other important element of narrative, plot, leads to the next question.

What Is the Shape of This Story?

Every piece of literature has some sort of structure, some skeleton on which the flesh hangs—some shape. For narrative, the shape is crucial, and that shape is determined by plot, which is the action of a story. We don't get to know the characters through much physical description (What do you think Nehemiah looks like?); we don't often get to know much about how they are feeling or reasoning; but we do get to see them (and hear them) in action. Plots in Old Testament narrative move along basically through scenes in which the characters speak and act.

The plot of a story usually (not always) includes these four elements:

1. Exposition (introduction)
2. Conflict (a problem or a tension in the story—and often a crisis)
3. Climax (a point of resolution, a high point, or a turning point in the story)
4. Conclusion (an endpiece, sometimes called denouement)

This is the general shape of a narrative. Think about the story of Little Red Riding Hood, for example:

1. Exposition: LRRH is sent by her mother to visit her grandmother.
2. Conflict: LRRH meets a big, bad wolf, who tricks her and her grandmother and eats them both (definitely a crisis!).
3. Climax: A good hunter arrives and cuts open the wolf, and out pop LRRH and her grandmother (definitely a resolution!).
4. Conclusion: LRRH goes safely back home to her mother.

It is important to say that we should not use this four-part structure as a rigid template into which we squeeze every narrative in the Bible in order to get the structure outlined. Some stories don't fit. In many cases, this shape (or sometimes part of it) is discernible and may help us see through to the structure of a narrative. In Nehemiah, after the briefest of expositions, the conflict bursts on the scene with the message brought by Hanani and the men from Judah. What is the climax of this book? Does the process of rebuilding the wall provide, in the midst of conflict, rising action that reaches a climax at the end of chapter 6, when the wall is finished? How, then, shall we view the second part of the book, chapters 7–12? Is the second part perhaps a second rebuilding, spiritual rather than physical, of people rather than of walls, through Word and Spirit as the visible focus rather than stones and swords, moving toward a spiritual climax in the dedication ceremony of chapter 12? What we can surely say is that the conclusion of chapter 13 brings not a settled resolution but rather renewed conflict—so that the plot is ultimately not resolved. Again, resolution is desperately needed—which is one of the points of this narrative.

Within the larger plot structure of a book like Nehemiah, each passage has its own unique structure that we must discern. What's the structure of the prayer in chapter 1, for example, and how is that prayer embedded into the telling of the story? (As Kathy Keller noted, it definitely postpones the physical action!) How is chapter 3, as Tim Keller pointed out, held together by "next to him" (or "after him") phrases—and what does that show us? How do the multiple episodes in the history of Israel recounted in chapter 9 repeatedly mirror the larger resolved and then unresolved plot of the whole book? Piper showed us this structure within chapter 9 and then took us to the larger context.

What Is the Context?

Of course, all these questions are related and work together. The question of context must join the mix sooner rather than later. Context simply means the words and the world that surround the passage. First of all, we must ask, for any text, how the texts on either side of it relate to it. For example, Nancy Guthrie and Carrie Sandom both asked why lists of names appear in Nehemiah (in chap. 7 and then in chap. 11), and how those lists relate to the action going on around them; this is important. I tried to show how the last section of chapter 12 makes sense logically in relation to the passages before and after. The larger context of any passage is the entire book in which it is found: it must find its place in the whole structure and flow of that book. The second part of

Nehemiah, the spiritual rebuilding, makes sense in relation to the first part, the physical rebuilding; each mirrors and sheds light on the other. Don Carson takes the final chapter of the book not as a free-standing episode, but truly as the conclusion to all that has gone before—which in one sense shows even more the bleakness of the narrative.

The *world* around a text is the historical context. The book of Nehemiah actually forces us to look into the historical context of these people who were called out by God; who were promised blessing, land, and a relationship with God through Abraham's seed; who grew into a great nation in the Land of Promise; who repeatedly rebelled despite the call of God's prophets and ultimately suffered the punishment of defeat and exile under the Babylonians (as God decreed); who are now a remnant returned to the land under Persian rule (as God promised); and who are rebuilding Jerusalem with its temple and sacrificial system as prescribed in God's Word. Not only is all this history found in the surrounding books of the Old Testament, but it also bleeds through the words and especially the prayers in the book of Nehemiah itself. The history of this people hangs heavy over this book from beginning to end.

But there's a larger context, of course—and without that larger context, the weight of this history and the ending of this book would be too heavy to bear. The next question we ask is not a separate question, because, as all these chapters have shown, implicit in this history that saturates the book are God's promises to his called-out people—promises of blessing for the nations from these people who are tracing Abraham's seed among themselves; promises of redemption for these people who look back and celebrate the redemption in Moses's time; promises of cleansing from sin anticipated by the blood sacrifices they're re-instituting in the temple; promises of an eternal King in David's line; and promises of God dwelling forever with his people in a holy city.

How Does This Story Relate to the Bible's Big Story of Redemption in Christ?

This is the question that puts every biblical narrative in the context of the Bible's overarching story. The only reason that most biblical narratives (and most stories in general) do reflect that four-part shape we summarized is that every story takes part in the big, true story of the universe. There is no other true story. It is the archetypal story:

1. Exposition: creation
2. Conflict: the fall
3. Climax: the cross and the resurrection
4. Conclusion: the consummation

The Bible's big story has Jesus Christ at the center—and at the beginning and the end. It is, at heart, a gospel story, a story of the Creator God providing a way out of the crisis of sin and death through the climactic sacrifice and resurrection of his Son on sinners' behalf, so that those sinners by faith are redeemed and dwell in the presence of God forever. The wonder of this amazing story is that it tells the truth; the God who authored it and himself entered it gives us his word on it.

The relation of Nehemiah (and of any Old Testament narrative) to the Bible's big story of redemption in Christ is not merely that we find in Nehemiah little hints of what Christ is like—although we may, and we may be encouraged by them. It's not that we can simply take the joy and unity we see at the high points of this story and explain that now we can have those things through Christ— although we can. Rather, as has been shown well in the chapters of this book, the relation of Nehemiah (and of any Old Testament narrative) to the Bible's big story of redemption in Christ is that it is actually part of that story—finding its place in that plot, sharing the same themes and the same trajectories toward the same end.

Nehemiah gives us the final elements of the Old Testament storyline within the larger story of God creating a people for himself through Jesus Christ. It takes place just on the brink of the intertestamental years leading up to Christ. The overarching story is not fully resolved because Christ has not yet come. It seems dark, on the brink of the light. The called-out people, from whom the Savior will come, desperately need the Savior in their sin and in their brokenness. But the book is full of gospel hope. God has brought them back to his temple and revived them through his Word. The revival is imperfect and the picture is dim, but the pieces are in place. Priests are ministering; sacrifices are being offered, pointing the way toward the final sacrifice for sin on the cross. At this point, by God's grace, his people are restored in the place where God will bring from their seed his own Son, come to die for their salvation—for *our* salvation. This is our story.

What's the Theme?

What is the story about? If we can aim for a one-sentence summary of what the story we are teaching is about, that summary can provide a guiding thesis for working out a teaching outline. I've put this question here, after the others, because, although it should work in our minds from the beginning, we are not ready to tackle it until we've thought deeply about the story, asking the questions we have covered so far—and probably more. Even then, our stated theme might change a bit the next time we come to study (or the next minute we think about it), as we see more in the text.

This question starts, obviously, at the level of the whole book. What is this book mainly about? Or, as a friend of mine likes to say, "What's the central thrust?" Or, as our friends at Proclamation Trust and Simeon Trust like to say, "What's the melodic line?"

So, what's the melodic line of Nehemiah? Having studied the two-part structure of Nehemiah, and having found matching processes of restoration, one physical and one spiritual, I was ready, when I wrote the commentary for chapter 6, to propose that Nehemiah is mainly about restoration. Fleshing that out, I might come up with something like this: *Nehemiah is about the restoration of a city and a people, according to God's faithful promises.* But further thinking tells me I might not want to land there: that proposed theme doesn't include the faithful response of Nehemiah, who is so central in this story. In another context, I've said that *the book is about God's faithfulness to his people and the call for their faithful response to him.* That seems accurate but a bit too general. Here's another stab: *Nehemiah faithfully leads God's people to restore God's city and to be restored around God's Word.* That's not bad. I'll keep working on it.

But even if I get that far, I'll be in better shape when called to teach the last section of chapter 12, for example, because I understand that passage falls in the second part, the part about being spiritually restored through the Word—and it comes at the end, as a kind of capstone on that section. So, might the central thrust of that little passage be to show the reinstitution of worship practices from the Law in order to keep the spiritual restoration going? We could be on our way.

All our nutshell themes and summaries are provisional stabs at articulating what we're understanding from Scripture. We must be as clear and faithful as possible, and always ready to learn more and see more—holding our insights and outlines loosely, with humility, submitting our thoughts and words to the authority of the Word. The context of the Bible's big redemptive story, with Christ at the center, should be always in our thoughts, always our reference point, always the story in which the one I'm reading finds its place and its ultimate meaning. The rebuilding of this city and this people leads to the Promised One who would come to this city, born of this people. That's what this story is pointing toward—and desperate for, at the end, in the context of all of Scripture. Should the book's theme be: *Nehemiah leads in the restoration of God's city and God's people according to God's Word—in anticipation of the final restoration to come only through God's Son?* Perhaps. That dark last chapter leads us toward an addition like that.

So What?

The first point to be made about this final question is that we must not forget to ask this question. How does an Old Testament narrative invade our hearts and lives, by the power of the Spirit, so that our lives are changed and Christ is glorified? Can a story do that?

We have been well warned these days against the danger of drawing moral lessons from a text without connecting that text to its gospel context. That is indeed a danger we must avoid. It is clear that the proper application of Nehemiah is not simply that we must aim to be like Nehemiah: faithful in leadership, prayerful, generous, diligent, and so forth. It is also clear that the true message of Nehemiah is not that, if we are like Nehemiah, we shall find success in the tasks we undertake: our walls will get built, and so on. It is also clear, as we have said, that the main message is not that Nehemiah was a lot like Christ.

I wonder if part of the problem with all of those examples is that they start with Nehemiah himself. What if we started with God? Davis recalls one of those good old gospel songs that went like this: "It is no secret what God can do; what he's done for others, he'll do for you." Davis suggests that we change the wording, due to the fact that things God has done for others he may actually *not* do for you. His suggestion: "What God *is* for others, he'll be for you." In reference to a story from the life of David, Davis concludes that our application of the text should be controlled not by David's situation but by "the character of David's God. That's where one always finds treasure."[5]

If it is true that Nehemiah's story participates in the Bible's big story of redemption in Christ, then we can find in this book just what our Redeemer God is like, how he relates to his people, and how he calls his people to relate to him—we can learn better how the big story goes! Certainly his sovereign hand on his people is a place to start—his sovereign hand that promises and works salva-

---

[5] Davis, *The Word Became Fresh*, 7.

tion, ultimately through his Son. His promises to accomplish that salvation are unfailing—the book of Nehemiah makes that clear. We should celebrate his mercy in protecting and restoring this people, as we are able to see the final outcome of that mercy on the cross for us sinners who could not save ourselves from sin and death. Through these chapters, we have truly celebrated who our faithful, redeeming God *is*—today, yesterday, and forever.

And certainly we can learn from this book about ourselves—as we see not what we must do to get something, but rather how our God has always called his people to respond to him: in faith, believing his Word, claiming his promises, praying to him wholeheartedly, worshiping and working with his people in obedience to his Word, and repenting and purifying our hearts and lives before him. Not only can we learn better how the story goes, we can also learn to live better and more faithfully in the story. God's ways have not changed, but we see them now fully revealed in Christ and accomplished in Christ. And we now respond to God empowered by the Spirit of the risen Christ in us. Surely, as we have been challenged by these sorts of applications, it has been the prodding of the Holy Spirit applying his Word, so that we might increasingly bring glory to the Lord Jesus we serve.

Glory in the Stories

We'll keep peering into these remarkable Old Testament narratives until Jesus comes again and the big story reaches its consummation. Then, without a doubt, all the little stories will be crystal clear as well. We will see how God the author and God the hero in all of them was shaping every detail of every plot for his good gospel purposes.

Meanwhile, may we keep telling the stories and teaching the stories of the Old Testament, so that through this part of the inspired Scriptures many will be drawn, many will be fed, and many will get the point, as John Piper says—the point that is a person, the Lord God who is making a name for himself.

Contributors

Paige Brown

After graduating from the University of Mississippi, Paige Brown completed a master's degree at Covenant Theological Seminary. She served with Reformed University Fellowship at Vanderbilt University and the University of Virginia, and as a teacher on staff at Park Cities Presbyterian Church (Dallas). Paige and her husband, Reagan, live in Nashville with their three children.

D. A. Carson

D. A. Carson (PhD, University of Cambridge) is cofounder and president of The Gospel Coalition and since 1978 has taught at Trinity Evangelical Divinity School (Deerfield, Illinois), where he currently serves as Research Professor of New Testament. He came to Trinity from Northwest Baptist Theological Seminary in Vancouver, British Columbia, and has served in pastoral ministry in Canada and the United Kingdom. He and his wife, Joy, have two children.

Nancy Guthrie

Nancy Guthrie speaks at conferences around the country and internationally, has authored numerous books, and hosts a podcast series, "Help Me Teach the Bible." She and her husband, David, live in Nashville. They are cohosts of the GriefShare video series used in more than eighty-five hundred churches around the country and host Respite Retreats for couples who have experienced the death of a child.

Kathy Keller

Kathy Keller holds an MA in theological studies from Gordon-Conwell Theological Seminary, has worked as an editor for Great Commission Publications, and presently serves on the staff of Redeemer Presbyterian Church in Manhattan, where her husband, Tim, is senior pastor. Kathy and Tim have three grown sons.

Tim Keller

Tim Keller serves as senior pastor of Redeemer Presbyterian Church in Manhattan. Originally from Pennsylvania, he was educated at Bucknell University, Gordon-Conwell Theological Seminary, and Westminster Theological Seminary. In 1989, Keller started Redeemer Presbyterian Church with his wife, Kathy, and their three sons. Keller is cofounder and vice president of The Gospel Coalition.

Kathleen Nielson

Kathleen Nielson (PhD, Vanderbilt University) is director of women's initiatives for The Gospel Coalition. She has taught English, directed Bible studies, speaks and writes extensively, and loves studying the Bible with women. Kathleen and her husband, Niel, live in Wheaton, Illinois, and have three sons, two daughters-in-law, and four granddaughters.

John Piper

John Piper (DTh, University of Munich) is founder and teacher of Desiring God (DesiringGod.org), and chancellor of Bethlehem College & Seminary in Minneapolis, Minnesota. He is a founding Council member of The Gospel Coalition. For thirty-three years, he served as senior pastor at Bethlehem Baptist Church. He and his wife, Noël, have four sons, one daughter, and a growing number of grandchildren.

Jenny Salt

Jenny Salt (MDiv, Trinity Evangelical Divinity School) is dean of students at Sydney Missionary and Bible College, where she has served since 1997. She shares her passion for expository Bible teaching and equipping in women's conferences throughout Australia, South Africa, and New Zealand. She loves enjoying time with family (including six nieces and nephews).

Carrie Sandom

Carrie Sandom (BTh, University of Oxford) serves as director of women's ministry for the Proclamation Trust in the UK and trains women for Bible teaching ministry at London's Cornhill Training Course. She worked with students in Cambridge and young professionals in London before moving to St. John's, Tunbridge Wells, where she works with women of all ages and stages of life.

General Index

Scripture Index

THE GOSPEL **COALITION**

The Gospel Coalition is a fellowship of evangelical churches deeply committed to renewing our faith in the gospel of Christ and to reforming our ministry practices to conform fully to the Scriptures. We have committed ourselves to invigorating churches with new hope and compelling joy based on the promises received by grace alone through faith alone in Christ alone.

We desire to champion the gospel with clarity, compassion, courage, and joy—gladly linking hearts with fellow believers across denominational, ethnic, and class lines. We yearn to work with all who, in addition to embracing our confession and theological vision for ministry, seek the lordship of Christ over the whole of life with unabashed hope in the power of the Holy Spirit to transform individuals, communities, and cultures.

Through its women's initiatives, The Gospel Coalition aims to support the growth of women in faithfully studying and sharing the Scriptures; in actively loving and serving the church; and in spreading the gospel of Jesus Christ in all their callings.

Join the cause and visit TGC.org for fresh resources that will equip you to love God with all your heart, soul, mind, and strength, and to love your neighbor as yourself.

TGC.org

Also Available from the Gospel Coalition

To see a full list of books published in partnership with the Gospel Coalition, visit crossway.org/TGC.